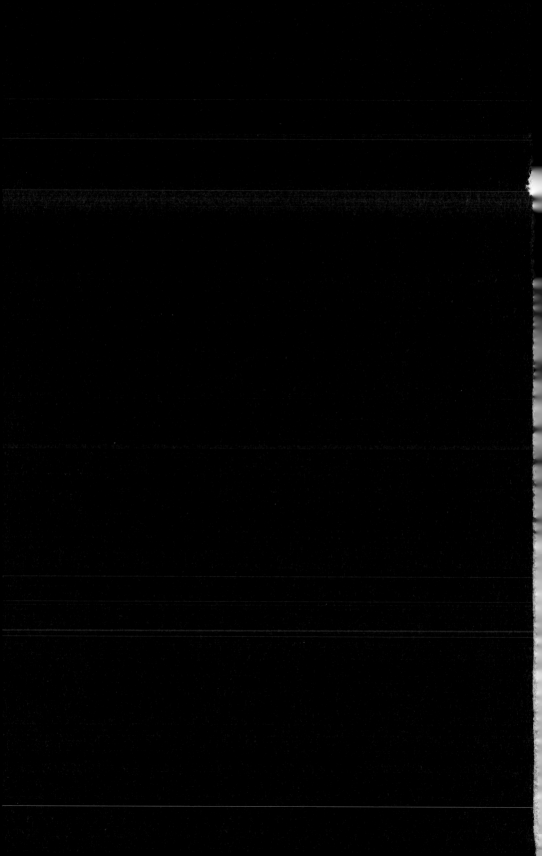

The Collected Works of
William Howard Taft

The Collected Works of
William Howard Taft

David H. Burton, General Editor

VOLUME II

POLITICAL ISSUES AND OUTLOOKS

SPEECHES DELIVERED BETWEEN

AUGUST 1908 AND FEBRUARY 1909

Edited with Commentary by

David H. Burton

OHIO UNIVERSITY PRESS

ATHENS

Ohio University Press, Athens, Ohio 45701
© 2001 by Ohio University Press
Printed in the United States of America
All rights reserved

Ohio University Press books are printed on acid-free paper ⊗ ™

09 08 07 06 05 04 03 02 01   5 4 3 2 1

Political Issues and Outlooks: Speeches Delivered between August 1908 and February 1909 published
New York: Doubleday, Page & Company, 1910.

Publication of *The Collected Works of William Howard Taft* has been made possible in part through the
generous support of The Louise Taft Semple Foundation of Cincinnati, Ohio, and the Earhart
Foundation of Ann Arbor, Michigan.

Frontispiece: Photograph of William Howard Taft as Secretary of War c. 1907–8 courtesy of
William Howard Taft National Historic Site

Library of Congress Cataloging-in-Publication Data

Taft, William H. (William Howard), 1857–1930.
    Political issues and outlooks : speeches delivered between August 1908 and February
1909 / by William Howard Taft ; edited with commentary by David H. Burton.
        p.   cm. — (The collected works of William Howard Taft ; v. 2)
    Includes bibliographical references.
    ISBN 0-8214-1395-3 (cloth : alk. paper)
    1. United States—Politics and government—1901–1909. 2. United States—Politics and
government—1909–1913. 3. Taft, William H. (William Howard), 1857–1930—Political
and social views. 4. Speeches, addresses, etc., American. I. Burton, David Henry, 1925–
II. Title.
E660 .T115 2001
973.9—dc21

Dedicated to
the Taft family,
for five generations serving
Ohio and the nation

The Collected Works of
William Howard Taft

David H. Burton, General Editor

VOLUME ONE
Four Aspects of Civic Duty and *Present Day Problems*
Edited with commentary by David H. Burton and A. E. Campbell

VOLUME TWO
Political Issues and Outlooks
Edited with commentary by David H. Burton

VOLUME THREE
Presidential Addresses and State Papers
Edited with commentary by David H. Burton

VOLUME FOUR
Presidential Messages to Congress
Edited with commentary by David H. Burton

VOLUME FIVE
Popular Government and *The Anti-Trust Act and the Supreme Court*
Edited with commentary by David Potash and Donald F. Anderson

VOLUME SIX
The President and His Powers and *The United States and Peace*
Edited with commentary by W. Carey McWilliams and Frank X. Gerrity

VOLUME SEVEN
Taft Papers on League of Nations
Edited with commentary by Frank X. Gerrity

VOLUME EIGHT
"Liberty under Law" and *Selected Supreme Court Opinions*
Edited with commentary by Francis Graham Lee
Cumulative Index

Contents

Commentary by David H. Burton, 1

1. The Federal Courts, 7
(Hot Springs, Virginia, August 6, 1908)

2. The Present Issues of the Two Great Parties, 19
(Hot Springs, Virginia, August 21, 1908)

3. The Republican View of Labor, 31
(Athens, Ohio, August 29, 1908)

4. Mr. Bryan's Claim to the Roosevelt Policies, 42
(Sandusky, Ohio, September 8, 1908)

5. The Future of the Negro, 52
(Cincinnati, Ohio, September 15, 1908)

6. In Defense of the Philippine Policy, 58
(Norwood, Ohio, September 19, 1908)

7. The Republican Party: What It Has Done, 68
(Cincinnati, Ohio, September 22, 1908)

8. The Railroads and the Courts, 85
(Chicago, Illinois, September 23, 1908)

9. A Pledge of Tariff Reform, 99
(Milwaukee, Wisconsin, September 24, 1908)

10. Postal Savings Banks and the Guaranty of Bank Deposits, 107
(St. Paul, Minnesota, September 28, 1908)

11. Labor and the Writ of Injunction, 122
(Topeka, Kansas, October 3, 1908)

12. The Debate of Lincoln and Douglass: A Look Backward, 126
(Galesburg, Illinois, October 7, 1908)

13. The Solid South and Its Political Past, 133
(Chattanooga, Tennessee, October 16, 1908)

14. Party Plans and Principles, 142
(Newark, New Jersey, October 19, 1908)

15. Mr. Gompers, the Courts and Labor, 153
(New York, New York, October 28, 1908)

16. A Few Words to Southern Democrats, 168
(Augusta, Georgia, January 14, 1909)

17. The Winning of the South, 172
(Atlanta, Georgia, January 15, 1909)

18. Hopeful Views of Negro Difficulties, 179
(Atlanta, Georgia, January 16, 1909)

19. The Young Men's Christian Association, 183
(Augusta, Georgia, January 17, 1909)

20. The Outlook of Negro Education, 194
(Augusta, Georgia, January 19, 1909)

21. The Uniting of Whites and Negroes, 199
(New Orleans, Louisiana, February 12, 1909)

22. The Learned Professions and Political Government, 204
(Philadelphia, Pennsylvania, February 22, 1909)

23. A Cheerful Review of Negro Activities, 216
(New York, New York, February 23, 1909)

Political Issues and Outlooks

Commentary

David H. Burton

Political Issues and Outlooks displays the critical thinking of William Howard Taft as he approached the presidency. The collection of speeches and writings contains numerous examples of Taft's mind in action, demonstrating again through early 1909 that Taft had something significant to say. Dealing with problems and issues, past and present, he spoke with knowledge and conviction. Statements made and positions taken were well thought out and often of considerable detail. In other words, the subjects he brought to the attention of the people and the manner in which they were developed show a sure understanding of public matters accompanied by a sincere desire to convince his audience and readers of his own commitment to the public good.

Many believed Taft would not excel at presidential campaigning, especially if the voters were to contrast his style with that of the outgoing president, Theodore Roosevelt, under whom he had served as vice president. Taft himself was heard to lament: "The next four months are going to be a night-mare for me." True, he was not a "natural" politician, but it is also important to differentiate style from substance. What Taft said from August to November 1908 gives a clear view of a mind that simultaneously focused on matters of concern to voters and offered something of lasting value. Not surprisingly, in one of his first stump speeches designed to recommend him to the electorate, and apart from the endorsement given him by President Roosevelt, he chose to take up issues surrounding the federal court system. Addressing the Virginia Bar Association, he brought up several matters of concern to judges and lawyers. He spoke, for example, of the unequal burden which delays and expense in the judicial system imposed on the poor litigant. "Sooner or later it is certain to rise and trouble us," he noted. In short, reform was in order. And it could come only through improvements in judicial procedure. What Taft went on to assert, in language no more legally abstruse than suited his audience, was his belief in equal justice for all. His conclusion is worth stressing: "We ought to be careful that professional conservatism does not keep us from equalizing justice as far as possible between the rich and the poor."

In several subsequent talks, Taft was generous in his praise of Roosevelt's accomplishments. He used the Roosevelt presidential record to underscore what he termed the "present issues" between the two major parties. This was obviously a good electioneering device. But Taft did admit to some failures to procure justice for the people over the previous twelve years of Republican rule. In itself this might be no more than a matter of practical candor. But, and here is a clue to his deeper, moral side, he saw these failures as attributable to "the fallibility of human nature and the willingness of ambitious and unscrupulous men to turn an instrumentality necessary in human progress to a vicious purpose." This was an unusual point to make in a political speech, especially when much of the address dealt with accusations of wrong-headed Democratic platforms from 1896 on. It suggests that even in the heat of political battle, Taft was able to think philosophically and was honest enough to share such thoughts as well.

One of the visionary proposals discussed by Taft in the 1908 campaign was a postal savings bank system. This pet project came to fruition in 1910, much to the president's satisfaction. In contrast, the Democratic platform called for a different kind of deposit guaranty. Bryan argued for government coverage of deposits in all the national banks, with the funds coming from a tax on each bank. For Taft, the Bryan proposal was a case of too much government involvement. Reflecting the thinking of the day, Taft called the Democratic approach "unjust, inequitable, and socialistic." "Socialistic" was a code word for un-American. When Taft thought of the postal savings bank, he had in mind individual investors placing small sums in what amounted to safe government accounts paying 2 percent interest. The investor was the tiny capitalist acting on his own for his own good. Here Taft was certainly in step with public opinion and popular culture. No less a social liberal than Oliver Wendell Holmes, Jr., was just such a fiscal conservative. As late as 1912, Holmes was heard to speak publicly to this effect: "It is not popular to tell the crowd that they have substantially all there is and that the war on capitalism is the fight of the striking group against all the other producers" (*Holmes-Sheehan Correspondence,* David H. Burton, ed. [Fordham University Press, 1993], p. 64). It appears that Taft was in very respectable intellectual company.

In later life, when Taft was asked to recall his most vivid memory of his education at Yale, without hesitation he replied that it was the teaching of William Graham Sumner.

A professor of political economy, Sumner was an avowed champion of Social Darwinism, powerful and strident in his declaration that the natural law, the law that must be obeyed, was survival of the fittest and death of the weakest so that the race could progress. He looked upon government efforts to ease the burdens of life as "the absurd effort to make the world over." If Taft came out of Yale a Social Darwinist of the Sumner persuasion, he steadily modified that belief and in the fullness of years stood forth as a moderate progressive with traces of Sumner's thought faint at best.

Social Darwinism has lent itself to various interpretations, modified by time and tide, among them "the white man's burden." Taft gave ample evidence of this during his years as the first civil governor of the Philippine Islands (1900–1904), a position in which he acquitted himself to the benefit of the Philippine people and his own reputation. By 1908, the anti-imperialists had been all but drowned out by America's humane administration of her island possessions, Puerto Rico and the Philippines. But such were Taft's sensitivity to criticism and pride of accomplishment that he chose to give a major address, "In Defense of the Philippine Policy," in September of the campaign year. As the former civil governor explained, the United States needed to do more than simply pacify the islands; it needed to prepare the people for self-government. To achieve peace and prosperity, a local constabulary must be empowered; a system of civil courts established; and schools, clinics, and roads built and maintained. All this, as Taft represented it, was the bounded duty of the United States. Thus a military victory due to American superiority over Spain, long sovereign in the Islands, took on a moral meaning. This moral tone dominated "In Defense of the Philippine Policy"; Sumner's philosophy of might as the ultima ratio was barely heard. If anything, it was might which made right prevail, the oft repeated justification of American expansion.

Taft is too-frequently dismissed as one who had no political sense. A survey of his most important campaign speeches reveals otherwise, at least in one daring particular. Theodore Roosevelt had long deplored the failure of the Republican party to make any inroads in the solidly Democratic South. He attempted in various ways, unsuccessfully as it turned out, to convince Southern voters to join the party of Lincoln. It fell to Taft to continue Roosevelt's initiatives. He proceeded to appeal to both white and black voters to support his candidacy. Speaking in his hometown, Cincinnati, he urged black Americans to find their rightful place in American society through education, not only in crafts and trades, but in health and legal professions as well. On another occasion, he called upon whites in Chattanooga to break with the Democratic party. His reasoning was simple: Southerners would be better served if they broke with tradition and voted Republican, thus joining forces with a party that had occupied the White House and dominated Congress for decades and whose platform benefited the South. Taft made a similar move when he congratulated the people of Augusta, Georgia by insisting that their conservatism was one of the underpinnings of the Constitution.

Regarding the cause of the Negro, Taft believed he would be on safe ground with Southern whites and blacks alike if he preached the gradualism of Booker T. Washington. He praised the black leader by name and expressed admiration for his work. As high-minded as Taft was, however, there were elements of condescension as he spoke of "latent defects" in the black race. At the same time, he was naive enough to believe that Southern society was "reaching the point" where the race problem would disappear. Taft was far more realistic when he treated such matters outside the South. In New York City some weeks after his election, he underscored the fact that there were ten million black people in the United States and argued that because they were not about to leave, it was time for all Americans to accept the reality of the black presence in American society. Taft the politician had taken it upon himself to face the race issue not squarely but at least obliquely. In so doing, he went further than would any president or presidential candidate down to Franklin Roosevelt in seeking the political support of a once-enslaved people.

1

The Federal Courts

Delivered before the Virginia Bar Association, at the Homestead Hotel,
Hot Springs, Virginia, August 6, 1908

The chief reason why the State devotes so much time and effort in the administration of justice is to promote the cause of peace and tranquillity in the community. Speaking theoretically and ideally, of course, our aim is to secure equal and exact justice; but practically, the object sought is peace.

The most recent instance of this was set forth most succinctly and forcibly in the able report of Governor Montague as to the progress in the establishment of a permanent tribunal at The Hague to settle international difficulties. While in theory this is to secure exact justice between the nations, practically its purpose is to avoid war.

In a Republic like ours, under popular control, with the dual form of government between the States and the United States, politico-legal questions which might tend to bring on conflict between parties and factions among the people were: first, the distribution of power under the Federal constitution between the National Government and the State governments; second, the division between the executive, the legislative and the judicial branches of the Government; and, third, the limitations upon governmental action either through the National Government or the State Government, in respect to the rights of individuals. Under our fundamental compact and its subsequent construction by the judicial branch, there was introduced a new and most effective instrument for the promotion of the peaceable settlement of those great governmental political controversies. The decisions in the cases of Marbury *v.* Madison and Cohen *v.* Virginia, which in their personal aspect took on the phase of a fundamental difference of opinion between two great Virginians, established the principle in this country, which has never been departed from, that the ultimate arbiter in respect to such great political and legal issues was and is the Supreme Court of the United States. It is true that this unique feature did not save us from the greatest civil war of modern times; but no one at all familiar with the history of the country can deny that this function of the Supreme Court of the United States and a similar one within the sphere of their jurisdiction of the Supreme Courts of the States, ultimately to decide upon the limitations of legislative and executive power, have greatly contributed to the peace and tranquillity of our community. This peculiar power of courts with us has carried their usefulness for the peaceful settlement of controversies beyond anything attempted in other countries. Of course, the exercise of this power must rest on the existence of a written constitution. Without it, there would be no guide for the courts except indefinite traditions that could hardly be made the basis for judicial decision. The power of the courts to declare invalid laws of the Legislature we know was not adopted without very bitter opposition; but I think the controversy was settled now so long ago that we generally agree that it has much contributed to the smooth working of our Constitution and to the supremacy of law and order in our community and offers great advantages over the methods of settling a similar class of questions in other countries.

While we may properly felicitate ourselves on this widened function of our courts, enabling us to avoid less peaceable methods of settling important politico-legal questions, have we the right to say that our present administration of justice generally insures continued popular satisfaction with its results? I think not. It may be true that down to the present time it has supplied a means of settling controversies between individuals and of bringing to punishment those who offend against the criminal laws sufficient to prevent a general disturbance of the peace and to keep the dissatisfied from violent manifestation against the Government and our present social system.

There are, however, abundant evidences that the prosecution of criminals has not been certain and thorough to the point of preventing popular protest. The existence of lynching in many parts of the country is directly traceable to this lack of uniformity and thoroughness in the enforcement of our criminal laws. This is a defect which must be remedied or it will ultimately destroy the Republic.

I shall not delay you this morning, however, with a discussion as to the reforms which ought to be adopted in the criminal branch of our jurisprudence. I have attempted this in an address on another occasion. I wish to confine myself to the delays and inequalities in the administration of justice in controversies between private persons, including, of course, corporations.

The present is a time when all our institutions are being subjected to close scrutiny with a view to the determination whether we have not now tried the institutions upon which modern society rests to the point of proving that some of them should be radically changed. The chief attack is on the institution of private property and is based upon the inequalities in the distribution of wealth and of human happiness that are apparent in our present system. As I have had occasion in other places to say frequently, I believe that, among human institutions, that of private property, next to personal liberty, has had most to do with the uplifting and the physical and moral improvement of the whole human race, but that it is not inconsistent with the rights of private property to impose limitations upon its uses for unlawful purposes, and that this is the remedy for reform rather than the abolition of the institution itself. But this scrutiny of our institutions, this increasing disposition to try experiments, to see whether there is not some method by which human happiness may be more equally distributed than it is, ought to make those of us who really believe in our institutions as essential to further progress, anxious to remove real and just ground for criticism in our present system.

I venture to think that one evil which has not attracted the attention of the community at large, but which is likely to grow in importance as the inequality between the poor and the rich in our civilization is studied, is in the delays in the administration of justice between individuals. As between two wealthy corporations, or two wealthy individual litigants, and where the subject-matter of the litigation reaches to tens and hundreds of thousands of dollars, where each party litigant is able to pay the expenses of litigation, large fees to counsel, and to undergo for the time being the loss of interest on the capital involved, our present system, while not perfect, is not so far from proper results as to call for anxiety. The judges of the country, both State and National, are good men. Venality in our judges is very rare; and while the standard of judicial ability and learning may not always be as high as we should like to see it, the provisions for review and for free and impartial hearing are such as generally to give just final judgments. The inequality that exists in our present administration of justice, and that sooner or later is certain to rise and trouble us, and to call for popular condemnation and reform, is the unequal burden which the delays and expense of litigation under our system impose on the poor litigant. In some communities I know, delays in litigation have induced merchants and commercial men to avoid courts altogether and to settle their controversies by arbitration, and to this extent the courts have been relieved; but such boards of arbitration are only possible as between those litigants that are members of the same commercial body and are in a sense associates. They offer no relief to the litigant of little means who finds himself engaged in a controversy with a wealthy opponent, whether individual or corporation.

The reform, if it is to come, must be reached through the improvement in our judicial procedure. In the first place, the codes of procedure are generally much too elaborate. It is possible to have a code of procedure simple and effective. This is shown by the present procedure in the English courts, most of which is framed by rules of court. The code of the State of New York is staggering in the number of its sections. A similar defect exists in some civil-law countries. The elaborate Spanish code of procedure that we found in the Philippines when we first went there could be used by a dilatory defendant to keep the plaintiff stamping in the vestibule of justice until time had made justice impossible. Every additional technicality, every additional rule of procedure adds to the expense of litigation. It is inevitable that with an elaborate code the expense of a suit involving a small sum is in proportion far greater than that involving a large sum. Hence it results that the cost of justice to the poor is always greater than it is to the rich, assuming that the poor are more often interested in small cases than the rich in large ones—a fairly reasonable assumption.

I listened with much pleasure to the discussion yesterday in respect to the proposed amendment to your procedure in Virginia, and I was reminded of a discussion of the same subject by that great lawyer, Mr. James C. Carter, of New York. He was the leader of the opposition to the New York code, and had to meet Mr. David Dudley Field, who was its chief supporter. Mr. Carter impressed me with having in that particular discussion the better side, for he showed that under the Massachusetts procedure, which is, I fancy, not unlike yours in Virginia, to wit, a retention of the common law forms of action, together with the division between law and equity, with modifications to dispense with the old technical niceties of common law and equity pleading, the decisions on questions of practice and pleading in Massachusetts were not one-tenth of those arising under the code of New York, and his argument was a fairly strong one in support of the contention which I heard here yesterday, that it was better to retain the old system and avoid its evils by amendment than to attempt a complete reform. However, it is to be said that a study of the English system consisting of a few general principles laid down in the practice act, and supplemented by rules of court to be adopted by the high court of judicature, has worked with great benefit to the litigant, and has secured much expedition in the settlement of controversies and has practically eliminated the discussion of points of practice and pleading in the appellate courts. My impression is that if the judges of the court of last resort were charged with the responsibility within general lines defined by the Legislature for providing a system in which the hearings on appeal should be solely with respect to the merits and not with respect to procedure, and which should make for expedition, they are about as well qualified to do this as anybody to whom the matter can be delegated.

This system of delegating questions of procedure to courts has a precedent of long standing in the Supreme Court of the United States, for under the Federal statutes that court has to frame the rules of equity to govern procedure in equity in the Federal courts of first instance. I may say, incidentally, that with deference to that great court, it has not given particular attention to the simplification of equity procedure and to the speeding of litigation in Federal courts which might well be brought about by a radical change in the rules of equity prescribed by it. It may be and probably is the fact that under the constitutional provision, Congress could not do away with the separation of law and equity cases as has been done in the codes of many of the States. I regret this because such a change makes for simplicity and expedition in the settlement of judicial controversies. It is clear, however, that the old equity practice could be greatly simplified. It has been done in England, and it ought to be done in the Federal courts.

One reason for delay in the lower courts is the disposition of judges to wait an undue length of time in the writing of their opinions or judgments. I speak with confidence on this point, for I have been one of the sinners myself. In English courts the ordinary practice is for the judge to deliver judgment immediately upon the close of the argument, and this is the practice that ought to be enforced as far as possible in our courts of first instance. It is of almost as much importance that the court of first instance should decide promptly as that it should decide right. If judges had to do so, they would become much more attentive to the argument during its presentation and much more likely on the whole to decide right when the evidence and arguments are fresh in their minds. In the Philippines we have adopted the system of refusing a judge his regular monthly stipend unless he can file a certificate, with his receipt for his salary, in which he certifies on honour that he has disposed of all the business submitted to him within the previous sixty days. This has had a marvelously good effect in keeping the dockets of the court clear.

It may be asserted as a general proposition, to which many legislatures seem to be oblivious, that everything which tends to prolong or delay litigation between individuals, or between individuals and corporations, is a great advantage for that litigant who has the longer purse. The man whose all is involved in the decision of the lawsuit is much prejudiced in a fight through the courts, if his opponent is able, by reason of his means, to prolong the litigation and keep him for years out of what really belongs to him. The wealthy defendant can almost always secure a compromise or yielding of lawful rights because of the necessities of the poor plaintiff. Many people who give the subject hasty consideration regard the system of appeals, by which a suit can be brought in a justice of the peace court and carried through the other courts to the Supreme Court, as the acme of human wisdom. The question is asked: "Shall the poor man be denied the opportunity to have his case re-examined in the highest tribunal in the land?" Generally the argument has been successful. In truth, there is nothing which is so detrimental to the interests of the poor man as the right which, if given to him, must be given to the other and wealthier party, of carrying the litigation to the court of last resort, which generally means two, three and four years of litigation. Could any greater opportunity be put in the hands of powerful corporations to fight off just claims, to defeat, injure or modify the legal rights of poor litigants, than to hold these litigants off from what is their just due by a lawsuit for such a period, with all the legal expenses incident to such a controversy? Every change of procedure that limits the right of appeal works for the benefit in the end of the poor litigant and puts him more on an equality with a wealthy opponent. It is probably true that the disposition of the litigation in the end is more likely to be just when three tribunals have passed upon it than when only one or two have settled it; but the injustice which meantime has been done by the delay to the party originally entitled to the judgment generally exceeds the advantage that he has had in ultimately winning the case. Generally in every system of courts there is a court of first instance, an intermediate court of appeals and a court of last resort. The court of first instance and the intermediate appellate court should be for the purpose of finally disposing in a just and prompt way all controversies between litigants. So far as the litigant is concerned, one appeal is all that he should be entitled to. The community at large is not interested in his having more than one. The function of the court of last resort should not primarily be for the purpose of securing a second review or appeal to the particular litigants whose case is carried to that court. It is true that the court can only act in concrete cases between particular litigants, and so incidentally it does furnish another review to the litigants, in that case; but the real reason for granting the review should be to enable the Supreme Court to lay down general principles of law for the benefit and guidance of the community at large. Therefore, the appellate jurisdiction of the court of last resort should be limited to those cases which are typical and which give to it in its judgment an opportunity to cover the whole field of the law. This may be done by limiting the cases within its cognizance to those involving a large sum of money, or to the construction of the Constitution of the United States or the States or their statutes. The great body of the litigation which it is important to dispose of, to end the particular controversies, should be confined to the courts of first instance and the intermediate appellate courts. It is better that the cases be all decided promptly, even if a few are wrongly decided.

In our supreme courts the business is disposed of with perhaps as great promptness as is consistent with the purposes of their jurisdiction. The criticism that courts of last resort are too much given to technicality has, I believe, some merit in it. Codes might be drawn, however, giving the courts of review more discretion in this matter than they now do by requiring the party complaining of an error in the trial court to show affirmatively that the result would have been different if the error had not been committed. The difference in importance between an error in the hurlyburly of the actual trial and in the calm of a court review under the urgent argument of counsel for plaintiff in error and the microscopic vision of an analytical but technical mind on the Supreme Bench is very great.

The complaints that the courts are made for the rich and not for the poor have no foundation in fact in the attitude of the courts upon the merits of any controversy which may come before them, for the judges of this country are as free from prejudice in this respect as it is possible to be. But the inevitable effect of the delays incident to the machinery now required in the settlement of controversies in judicial tribunals is to opppress and put at a disadvantage the poor litigant and give great advantage to his wealthy opponent. I do not mean to say that it is possible, humanly speaking, to put them on an exact equality in regard to litigation; but it is certainly possible to reduce greatly the disadvantage under which the man of little means labours in vindicating or defending his rights in court under the existing system, and courts and legislatures could devote themselves to no higher purpose than the elimination from the present system of those of its provisions which tend to prolong the time in which judicial controversies are disposed of.

The shortening of the time will reduce the expense, because, first, the fees of the lawyers must be less if the time taken is not so great. Second, the incidental court fees and costs would be less.

Again, I believe that a great reform might be effected, certainly in the

Federal courts, and I think too in the State courts, by a mandatory reduction of the court costs and fees. In the interest of public economy we have generally adopted a fee system by which the officers of the courts are paid. Human nature has operated as it might have been expected to operate, and the court officers, the clerk and the marshal, have not failed, especially in the Federal courts, to make the litigation as expensive as possible, with a view to making certain the earning of a sufficient amount to pay their salaries. The compensation of the officers of the court and the fees charged ought to be entirely separate considerations. The losses which the Government may have to suffer through the lack of energy in the collection of costs and fees should be remedied in some other way. The salaries of the court officers should be fixed and should be paid out of the treasury of the county, state or national government, as the case may be, and fees should be reduced to as low a figure as possible consistent with a reasonable discouragement of groundless and unnecessary litigation. I believe it is sufficiently in the interest of the public at large to promote equality between litigants, to take upon the Government much more than has already been done, the burden of private litigation. What I have said has peculiar application to the Federal courts. The feeling with respect to their jurisdiction has been that, limited as it is now to cases involving not less than $2,000, the litigation must, of course, be between men better able to undergo its expense than in cases involving a lesser amount, and therefore that high fees and costs are not so objectionable in those courts as in the State courts. I think this has been a very unfortunate view and has been one of the several grounds for creating the prejudice that has undoubtedly existed in popular estimation against the Federal courts as rich men's courts. In those courts suits for damages for personal injury, of which many are there by removal of defendant, are generally brought by poor persons. Then the expense of litigation in patent cases is almost prohibitive for a poor inventor. It forces him into contracts that largely deprive him of the benefit of his invention. In respect to patent cases much might be done by the Supreme Courts reforming the equity procedure and the bill of costs.

I think another step in the direction of the dispatch of litigation would be the requirement of higher qualifications for those judges who sit to hear the cases involving a small pecuniary amount. The system by which the justices of the peace who have to do with smaller cases and who are non-professional men and not apt in the disposition of business, is hardly a wise feature of the present system. The poor should have the benefit of as acute and able judges as the rich, and the money saved in the smaller salaries of the judges of the inferior courts is not an economy in the interest of the public. Under able, educated and well-paid judges who understand the purpose of the law in creating them, I am quite sure that the people's courts, as they are called, could be made much more effective than they are for the final settlement of controversies.

Another method by which the irritation at the inequalities in our administration of justice may be reduced is by the introduction of a system for settling of damage suits brought by employees against public service corporations through official arbitration and without resort to jury trials. Such a system is working in England, as I am informed. Under the statute, limitations are imposed upon the recovery of the employee or his representatives proportioned to his earning capacity. The hearing is prompt and the payment of the award equally prompt, and in this way a large mass of litigation that now blocks our courts would be taken out of our judicial tribunals, and be settled with dispatch. Of course it would not be proper or possible to prevent the plaintiff litigant from resorting to a jury trial if he chooses, but I believe that the result would be very largely to reduce the character of such litigation. The truth is that these suits for damages for injuries to employees and passengers and to trespassers and licensees have grown to be such a very large part of the litigation in each court, both in courts of first instance and in courts of appeal, and involve so much time because of the necessity for a jury trial, that they may be properly treated as a class, and special statutory provision for their settlement by arbitration or otherwise be made. These are the cases which create most irritation against the courts among the poor. This is peculiarly true in such cases in the Federal courts.

No one can have sat upon the Federal Bench as I did for eight or nine years and not realize how defective the administration of justice in these cases must have seemed to the defeated plaintiff, whether he was the legless or armless employee himself or his personal representative. A non-resident railway corporation had removed the case which had been brought in the local court of the county in which the injured employee lived, to the Federal court, held, it may be, at a town forty or one hundred miles away. To this place at great expense the plaintiff was obliged to carry his witnesses. The case came on for trial, the evidence was produced and under the strict Federal rule as to contributory negligence or as to non-liability for the negligence of fellow-servants, the judge was obliged to direct the jury to return a verdict for the defendant. Then the plaintiff's lawyer had to explain to him that if he had been able to remain in the State court, a different rule of liability of the company would have obtained, and he would have recovered a verdict. How could a litigant thus defeated, after incurring the heavy expenses incident to litigation in the Federal court, with nothing to show for it, have any other feeling than that the Federal courts were instruments of injustice and not justice, and that they were organized to defend corporations and not to help the poor to their rights. I am glad to be able to say that under the Interstate Commerce Employers' Liability Act much of this occasion for bitterness against the Federal courts and their administration of justice will be removed, and I believe it would greatly add to the popular confidence in the Federal courts if a Federal statute were enacted, by which, under proper limitations, official arbitration could be provided for settling the awards to employees in such cases arising in the carrying on of interstate commerce. We cannot, of course, dispense with the jury system. It is that which makes the people a part of the administration of justice and prevents the possibility of government oppression, but every means by which in civil cases litigants may be induced voluntarily to avoid the expense, delay and burden of jury trials ought to be encouraged, because in this way the general administration of justice can be greatly facilitated and the expense incident to delay in litigation can be greatly reduced.

I listened with professional pride yesterday, as every lawyer must have done, to the deserved encomiums which Senator Lindsay paid to the members of our profession and their willing sacrifices in every crisis in our country's history. Certainly no one has a profounder admiration than I have for the important part which the members of our profession must play in making a permanent success of self-government. I venture to suggest, however, that in respect to these details of our profession, these technicalities out of which can grow real abuses, there is sometimes a disposition on the part of the members of our profession to treat litigants as made for the courts and the lawyers, and not the courts and lawyers as made for litigants. As it is lawyers who in judicial committees of the legislature draft the codes of procedure, there is not as strong an impelling force as there ought to be to make the final disposition of cases as short as possible.

There is a story among the traditions of our Ohio Bar that a Mr. Nash, who had written a book generally used to aid practitioners in Ohio before the adoption of the code of procedure in 1851, was very indignant at the enactment of that new measure, and he severely condemned it. He said that the code was a barbarous arrangement under which a suit could be brought against one man, judgment taken against another and an execution issued upon that judgment against any good man in the State of Ohio. Now our profession is naturally conservative. It is our natural disposition to have things done in an orderly way and to believe that the way in which things have been done should not be departed from until we clearly see an opportunity for improvement. I do not object to this spirit. Especially in this country, I think there will be progressive movements sufficient to prevent such conservatism from being a real obstruction to our general progress. I venture to think, however, that in the matter of procedure and in the adoption of special methods and systems for the settling of classes of controversies, we ought to be careful that this professional conservatism does not keep us, with the power that we necessarily exercise in respect to technical legal legislation, from adopting the reforms which are in the interest of equalizing the administration of justice as far as possible between the rich and the poor.

2

The Present Issues of the Two Great Parties

Delivered at Hot Springs, Virginia, August 21, 1908

Fellow-Republicans, Citizens of Virginia, Ladies and Gentlemen:

I came into this beautiful country after a strenuous year, in order that I might have rest and exercise and thereby gain health and strength. I had not intended to bring politics into this neighborhood. I had hoped that all that might be postponed until I reached my home in Cincinnati; but I have yielded to the kindly and pressing invitation of the local Republican leaders that I meet the earnest and enthusiastic members of the party in the neighboring mountain counties of Virginia and say something to them in a summary and general way of the present issues between the two great parties.

The last Democratic Administration entered upon its labors in March, 1893, and gave up power, under the mandate of the people, in March, 1897. During this period, it repealed the McKinley Tariff Bill, passed in 1890, and enacted the Gorman-Wilson Tariff Bill of 1893. With the prospect of a Democratic tariff for revenue and under the operation of the Gorman-Wilson Tariff Bill subsequently passed, a period of industrial depression set in, which continued through the next Presidential campaign of 1896.

The remedy for this depression as proposed by the Democratic party under its present leadership was a change from the gold standard of currency and values, which was the measure of all pecuniary obligations, to a silver standard—a change which would have scaled the debts of all by quite 50 percent, and would have produced a financial crash in which the business disaster would only have been exceeded by the injury to our national financial honor.

As soon as the Republican party came into power in 1897, it repealed the Gorman-Wilson Tariff Bill, and enacted the present Dingley Tariff Bill. The maintenance of the financial honor of this country, the assurance of an honest monetary standard, and the operation of the new tariff led to such confidence in the business community and encouraged so widely the investment of capital, that from 1897 to 1907 there followed a period of business expansion and a prosperity never before known in the history of the world. Wages were never higher and the average standard of living of the wage earners, of the farmers and of the business men, in point of comfort and enjoyment of life, was advanced beyond precedent. Incident to this tremendous material progress, however, there crept in abuses growing out of the fallibility of human nature, of the dishonesty of some prominent men entrusted with the management of the business of others and of a greed of financial power of some stimulated by the enormous successes incident to the combination of capital in large corporations. The abuses chiefly took the form of the violation of the Antitrust Law directed against monopolies of interstate commerce and of the granting of rebates and discriminations by railways to large shippers. The extent to which these evils had grown was not brought home to the people, whose attention had been absorbed in the prosperity of the country and in the problems arising in the Spanish War and in the new responsibilities which followed it, until early in the present Administration, when revelations, the result of official investigations by State and National authority, showed them that a condition had arisen which called for a halt and for the adoption of some method of supervising interstate commerce carried on by railroads and great industrial corporations which should keep these instrumentalities within the law. It was then that Theodore Roosevelt, who had been elected President in 1904, invoked the attention of Congress and the public to these abuses and asked for remedial legislation, and by exercise of the executive power took prompt steps himself to secure a more thorough enforcement of the laws then on the statute books than up to that time had been achieved. The Republican party had enacted the Antitrust Law as far back as 1890; but the law was general in its terms and needed the slow course of judicial construction to make effective its mandate and to enable both prosecuting officers and persons within its operation to understand the exact limitations that it imposed. It had enacted the Interstate Commerce Law and its amendment by the Elkins Bill, to make more efficient the prosecutions of railway rebates and discriminations, but successful prosecutions had not yet been had under them.

It is true that from time to time the platforms of both parties had invited attention to the danger from the misuse and abuse of the combinations of capital in maintaining illegal monopolies. It was not, however, until Mr. Roosevelt, realizing to the full the danger to which our society was exposed, unless the offending corporations, railway and industrial, were made to obey and fear the law, took vigorous action in the recommendation of new legislation and in the enforcement of the old, that anything very effective was done to check the growing evil. He directed many prosecutions both under the Antitrust Law and the Interstate Commerce Law, and extended investigation by the Departments of Commerce and Labor, and of Justice, into the cooperation of railways and industrial combinations in the maintenance of secret rebates and discriminations. He developed the fact that the chief instrument for the maintenance of illegal industrial monopolies was the rebate system. He called on the Republican Congress, which had been elected with him in 1904, and nobly did that Congress respond. It made a record for remedial legislation along the lines recommended by him which, as he has himself said, has never been equaled in our time. The Railway Rate Bill, the bill creating the Bureau of Corporations, the Pure Food Bill, the Meat Inspection Bill, were all measures framed for the purpose of stamping out the abuses which had grown up in the conduct of business by some corporations that were flouting the law and the interests of the public. Most of these measures were considered in the last session of the Congress elected in 1902, and encountering the open, bitter opposition of all the corporations affected by them, failed of passage. They were introduced in the next Congress, and in spite of the continued opposition, in spite of the influence which it was charged such corporations must have because of alleged campaign contributions to the Republican party, the measures were triumphantly adopted. What has been the result of this legislation and executive action? Secret rebates and unlawful discriminations have been actually abolished. No monopoly of business in any line is now maintained by a secret reduction of freight rates to it which is denied to competitors. All combinations are diligently consulting the law. The fear of the statute and its penalties has been put in the hearts of its former violators. A great step has been taken and, despite the opposition of corporate interests, the moral awakening of the people has found expression in the adoption of great legislative measures and the vigorous execution of them by a Republican Congress and a Republican President. The people have ruled through the Republican party. Not only have the Republican President and Congress thus struck a staggering blow to the abuses to which I have referred and taken a long step toward their reform, but they have also, in the face of corporate opposition, passed measures of the utmost importance in putting the employees of capital invested in interstate commerce on a level in respect to the liabilities growing out of the contract of employment. I have no hesitation in saying that not since the beginning of the Government has any other national administration done so much for the cause of labor by the enactment of remedial legislation as Theodore Roosevelt and the Republican Congresses elected and sitting during his terms of office.

It is true that additional legislation is needed to perfect the machinery for enforcing the principles laid down by Mr. Roosevelt and declared in the remedial statutes already passed so as to clinch the progress already made and to insure further progress. It is also true that Mr. Roosevelt has made recommendations for some of such needed legislation which has not been enacted by the present Congress into law. The present Congress has furnished the money for the enforcement of the remedial statutes of the previous Congress and has provided an increase of civil servants needed to execute them and in so doing has drawn down upon it the denunciation of the Democratic platform. This Congress has reënacted the Employers' Liability Act, has strengthened the Safety Appliance Acts, has passed the Government Employees' Compensation Act, has directed investigation into mine disasters and has passed a model Child Labor Bill. It has not amended the Interstate Commerce Law so as to prevent over-issue of stocks and bonds on interstate railroads and it has not amended the Antitrust Law as suggested by Mr. Roosevelt. The failure of Congress at once to adopt executive recommendations on such a subject is not justifiable ground for supposing that either the same Congress, or a succeeding one under the same party control, will not in due course adopt some proper legislative remedies for the defects in existing legislation. The failure of the rate bill in one Republican Congress was followed by its passage in a much more drastic and effective form by the next one. As Mr. Roosevelt himself has said, "Congress must take account not of one national need but of many and widely different national needs. . . . No Congress can do everything; still less can it in one session meet every need."

The abuses to which I have referred, due to the misuse of combinations of capital, are a development in our body politic and social requiring a limitation upon the use of property and capital such as to prevent the evils described on the one hand and to interfere with the institution of private property and the maintenance of a motive for individualism and thrift as little as possible on the other. The evil to be avoided is not one which yields to hastily formed or vaguely described statutes suggested in the hurry of a political campaign or approved for the purpose of catching votes. It involves a careful study of the operation of detailed provisions of law; it involves a knowledge of the difficulties of criminal prosecution under our present system; it requires a consideration of the line between National and State jurisdiction and also of the extent of the Federal power under the interstate commerce clause of the Constitution; and it will doubtless require, before the reform is sufficiently broad and effective, a series of amendments suggested by actual experience of earnest men engaged in a sincere effort to reach the real guilty without involving the punishment of the innocent, of striking down the abuses of the law-defying wealthy and at the same time preserving to thrift and industrial enterprise the rewards essential to continued material progress.

The fact that the Democratic party had but little recent experience in the responsibilities of power and but little training in actual legislation, makes the party and its distinguished leader oblivious of the necessity for care and caution in the enactment of statutes which are to accomplish changes in our social and business relations. They seem to have an impression that an evil which is very insidious, and which is elusive in its character when definite legal description is to be given of it and heavy penalty is to be prescribed for it, may be safely met by a statutory denunciation hastily prepared in a day or a week or a short period. We have seen within the four short years of the present Administration, such measures as government ownership of railways, election of Federal judges and National initiative and referendum proposed as remedies for our existing evils and now withdrawn under assurances that they will not be again suggested. May we, therefore, not regard the inaction of one session of Congress as deliberation in a matter requiring it rather than as a basis for the claim that the Legislature wishes to defeat the will of the people? The truth is we are dealing with an incident of human progress and with some unfavorable condition produced by the operation of individualism and the institution of private property which it will require all the practical common sense of the American people exercised in the passage of statute after statute properly to meet without placing obstacles in the way of true progress. The suggestion that they ought to be fully met and completely corrected by an administration in a short four years could come from no one who has a full appreciation of the difficulty of permanently stamping out such evils by statutory law and its enforcement.

The claim is now made that the Republican party is responsible for the abuses I have described and that with its control of the Government for the last twelve years, its failure to remedy them requires its deposition from power. The evils were due to the fallibility of human nature and the willingness of ambitious and unscrupulous men to turn an instrumentality necessary in human progress to a vicious purpose. A party is responsible for evils thus arising only when it fails to correct them after they become known. I have already pointed out that the Republican party long ago passed the Antitrust Law and is vigorously enforcing it. I have already stated that it passed the Interstate Commerce Law and its amendments, the Elkins Law and the Rate Bill, and is vigorously enforcing them. I have already dwelt on the great change for the better that has thus been brought about by this Administration. I have said that the extent of the abuses was not known or realized during the time when the burden of the Spanish War and its consequences had to be met, or until revelations were made early in this Administration when the work of remedying them was at once begun.

If these abuses were always well known, as now claimed, and the necessity for their radical and drastic reform was clear to all and especially to the Democratic party under its present leadership, it would seem that of all the possible agencies for reform, the Democratic party is the one least entitled to any credit. For while the resolutions of its platforms in 1896, 1900 and 1904 denounced the abuses of corporate wealth, they never proposed feasible plans, or made the prominent and chief issue of any campaign the carrying out of what have now become known, and properly known, as the Roosevelt policies. On the contrary, in 1896, the party made the chief issue a disastrous financial experiment which would have retarded the progress of this country a quarter of a century and sullied its financial honor. In 1900 the party reiterated its adherence to this suicidal policy of repudiation of National and private debts and obligations, and then advanced as the paramount issue of the campaign, not the trusts, not corporate wealth and abuses, but rather the repudiation of all our international responsibilities growing out of the Spanish War and the destruction of what they called the growing cancer of imperialism in the policy of this country. Again in 1904, instead of selecting the abuses and evils for which they now seek to make the Republican party responsible, as the main issue of the campaign, the burden of their contention was the usurpation of the powers of the executive office by President Roosevelt, including his settlement of the anthracite coal strike and the violation of the Federal constitutional limitations by the Republican party, while the extent of the trust evil was minimized by the statement of the then party candidate that the common law furnished sufficient remedy to suppress it and by the general party declaration that nothing but safe and sane policies were to be adopted under the Administration which should follow its success in the election. The people, in 1896, by a substantial majority, rejected the plan of repudiation of the Democratic party. In 1900 the people again by even a greater majority rejected the plan of the Democratic party to repudiate the National responsibilities; and in 1904 they again rejected the same party which had temporarily assumed its ancient character as a preserver of the Constitution. This is the record of the party whose policies it is claimed Mr. Roosevelt and the Republican party have stolen, in the actual abolition of railway rebates and discriminations, in the active enforcement of the Antitrust Law, in the passage of a pure food law, in the passage of a meat inspection law, and in the actual demonstration that corporate interests and influences do not control the passage of laws or the enforcement of them under the present Republican Administration.

But it is said that the people do not rule in this country. My impression has always been that the election of Mr. McKinley and a Republican Congress, in 1896, was one of the most intelligent and effective expressions of popular will ever manifested to the world, and that the maintenance of the gold standard and a protective tariff by his Administration was a correct interpretation of the people's will. This was conclusively shown to be so by even a greater majority for Mr. McKinley in 1900. When Theodore Roosevelt was chosen in 1904, a still greater majority was returned, and the inference that he and the Republican Congress under him had again carried out the people's will was indisputable. We may well submit to the country whether his present Administration has not expressed the will of the people in the Roosevelt policies.

It is suggested that the popular will is to be suppressed because the Speaker of the House of Representatives will be given certain powers in the procedure of the House if Republican. I do not intend to enter into a discussion of the wisdom of such procedure. Suffice it to say, that at one end of the Capitol we have the example of a body that has no rule for the previous question, and in which the ability of the minority to defeat or delay legislation favored by the majority has been made the subject of criticism on the ground that this defeated the will of the people. The House of Representatives is a much larger body in which no business at all could be done unless the rules in some way secure control to the majority over the business to be done, and stricter rules of procedure have been adopted. The rules cannot be adopted or amended except by a majority of the people's chosen representatives. Whether such rules might well be modified or not, it suffices to meet the criticism of our Democratic friends to say that the rules complained of, which were originally adopted under Speaker Reed for the purpose of doing business in the House, were subsequently adopted by a Democratic House for the same purpose.

But whatever may be thought of the House procedure, there is not the slightest doubt that after the present campaign, after the declaration by the Republican National Convention that the Roosevelt policies are to be followed, after the specific promise made by the National Convention to render more effective the provisions of the Anti-trust Law, and the Interstate Commerce Law, by restricting the overissue of stocks and bonds on interstate railroads, that a Republican Congress when elected can be counted on to take up and, with due consideration of the form and details of the proposed measures, adopt the remedies promised with the same loyalty to the popular will as the Republican Congress elected with Mr. Roosevelt manifested in the enactment of the most important statutes that have been placed upon the statute books in our time for the suppression of economic evils.

I wish to speak for a little while upon the Republican and Democratic parties in the South. The situation with respect to the present national issue in the South is most peculiar. It is not too much to affirm that a great number of Democrats are opposed to the Democratic party under its present leadership. Of these, many will vote for the nominee of the party; many of them will not vote at all, and a considerable number will vote for the Republican nominee. Yet none of them will be disappointed if the Democratic ticket is defeated.

Everyone having the interest of the country at heart, as an abstract proposition, would rejoice to have the Solid South as a Democratic asset in every National campaign broken up. It would be better for the States themselves; it would be better for the country. The Republican party is not the sectional party which the fact that the South always supports the Democratic party would indicate. The Republican party has improved the waterways, is building the Panama Canal, and has started the movement for the reclamation of swamp lands, the conservation of forest and water resources, and is taking many other steps that are for the development of the South. The growth and success of the mining and iron industries in the South are directly due to laws enacted by the Republican party. In our dependencies when offices have had to be filled in the Philippines, Porto Rico and Cuba, no attention has been paid to the partisan proclivities of the appointees, and there are today in the Philippines as many Democrats among the Americans as Republicans serving the Government there.

Leading Democrats from the South have complained, and with much ground, that the leading men of the South have but little influence in the executive branch of the Government at Washington, and as the executive branch is always in action, is always on guard, and has much to do with framing the foreign and domestic policies of the country, this makes the South feel that it is not exercising its share of national government control. The reason is that the South has always been considered by the Democracy, and especially the Northern Democracy, as a part of the country certain to support the Democratic ticket, and therefore when the Republican party is in power, it is not either natural or to be expected that it should summon to its Executive the leading men from the opposing party in the South. The only way by which the South can cure this matter is by independence of action and the support of the Republican ticket.

I know the South is a conservative portion of the country. By tradition, its attachment to the Democratic party is firm; but a party represents principles, and when the principles change, though the name of the party remain the same, it would seem that after a while the traditional attachment to party would rest lightly on an intelligent community. Still there is a political habit, a political association which a conservative people hesitates to throw off.

Many independent Democrats in the South agree with the Republican party in all its main economic doctrines. Since 1890 the manufacturing interests of the South have exceeded her agricultural interests; the industrial expansion of the South exceeds that of any other part of this country, and is really the marvel of the world. Its cotton manufactures, its iron manufactures have grown enormously, and the South is today in its cotton factories, in its iron factories and in the sugar culture of Louisiana more dependent for its business prosperity on the maintenance of a reasonable protective tariff than any other community in the country. It is vitally interested that the coming revision of the tariff shall be made upon protective principles and not with a view to the adoption of a revenue tariff.

The Spanish War led to the entering of the flower of the young men of the South into the army of the United States in order to uphold the country's cause. This did much to remove sectional feeling lingering after the Civil War and served to unite in a common brotherhood the blue and the gray. Many of the Southern Democrats have taken an active interest in promoting our present Philippine policy and more are in sympathy with it. They are opposed to the policy of scuttling out of the Philippines; they generally believe that we have a problem of national responsibility there of aiding those people to stand upon their own feet, and that we ought not to leave the islands until we have fully completed our work. They rejoice in the missionary character of what we are doing, and in the spread of Christian civilization that we are helping on by our policy in the Philippines.

So, too, they have not the slightest sympathy with that spirit of the Democratic platform favoring a destruction of certain industrial interests for the purpose of stamping out the evil in their conduct rather than their regulation, with a view to bringing them within the law. They know and understand the threat against the prosperity of the country involved in placing in power the Democratic party under its present leadership.

We hear much of Jeffersonian Democracy and the adherence by the present régime of the Democratic party to the principles of Thomas Jefferson. I venture to say that if Jefferson were to return to life, he would not recognize his reputed political descendants. While there is a good deal of declaration in the Denver platform against centralization of power, the propositions contained in the Democratic platform are even more Federalistic in their tendency than those in the Republican platform. The Republican party has always been in favor of a liberal construction of the Constitution to maintain the national power, and its attitude in this regard might in times past have justified a Southern Democrat in assuming that there was at least one principle left of the old Democracy to which he might adhere by voting the Democratic ticket; but that resource in the present Denver platform has been completely eliminated and propositions are there made which the most Federalistic statesman might find it very difficult to work out under the Federal Constitution.

It is the duty of the Republicans of the South to take advantage of this mental attitude I have described on the part of many independent Democrats. How can they take such advantage? They can do so by thorough organization of their party and an effort to secure votes in November for the National, Congressional and State tickets. They should put forward for office good men, men of high character, and by their energy in the election contest avoid the criticism that the Republican party in the South is organized merely for the purpose of receiving Federal patronage. They should show that it is a real political party, determined to discuss the issues and to attract into its ranks the men who sympathize with the fight they are making, but who are as yet, because of tradition, reluctant to join them openly in the fight. This fight should be made without regard to whether we can gain the electoral vote of any Southern State. The present is an opportunity that ought not to be lost, for if it is improved, if the Republicans of the South by active organization, and with the sympathy of many independent Democrats, can increase their votes this year substantially, it means a great step toward the subsequent relief of the Southern States from the political thraldom of the past. I know what a burden Southern Republicans have had to carry. I know the courage it has taken for them to remain Republicans when their cause seemed hopeless. But I believe a change is coming.

I congratulate you Republicans of Virginia on the auspicious beginning of this campaign. I congratulate you that within your own boundaries are many Democrats who are looking forward with the hope that you may succeed, and I beg of you, in your methods and in the men that you put up for office, to demonstrate that there is in this State a reputable Republican party with which independent Democrats may be glad to ally themselves. The presence here of so many intelligent, earnest and enthusiastic Republicans itself furnishes such a demonstration.

3

The Republican View of Labor

Delivered before the Taft Club of Athens, Ohio, August 29, 1908

My Friends:

When I say that it is an unexpected pleasure for me to address you I think you will believe me. I had hoped that I might go through Ohio with a single speech at Athens, a speech appreciative of the soldiers' reunion here, without going into politics or a general discussion at all. The truth is, I am not much of a politician. I haven't had a great deal of experience in it, and I feel very deeply the responsibility that I have upon me now as the candidate of a great party, lest I may not fill the measure that the members of that party are entitled to have filled by one who proposes to hold their banner temporarily and to lead them on to victory, and I am from time to time oppressed with the sense that I am not the man who ought to have been selected, and yet, my friends, I am not going to decline.

We are in a four years' campaign. The question is whether the mandate of power shall be given again to the Republican party, or shall be turned over to the Democratic party; to the Republican party now led by Theodore Roosevelt as President of the United States, or to the Democratic party led by Mr. Bryan, who has twice before been a candidate of that party before the people of the United States. In making a selection of your servants, your agents, of those who are to do your work, you ordinarily test the question whom you shall select by what they have done in the past, and if there be a party in power that has specifically met with efficiency and success the problems to be solved, the conclusion you will come to is that that party ought to be continued, rather than that another party should be put in power, whose policy you may be uncertain about, and whose efficiency in the administration of any policy you may still be more uncertain about. I venture to say that never in the history of the country has there been an Administration which has had more problems to meet, that has met them with more certainty and efficiency than the Administration under the Republican party by Theodore Roosevelt, and previously under William McKinley with the same party.

The Spanish War was met and fought under the control of William McKinley, and with the majority of the Republican party in both Houses of Congress. The questions with respect to the Philippines and Cuba which followed that war were met again by that party, and I ask you, gentlemen, whether any scandal, whether any charge of inefficiency has been established in the discharge of the new responsibilities that the Republican party was obliged to assume under William McKinley and Theodore Roosevelt?

Then there came the question whether we should build the Isthmian canal and unite the two great oceans. Mr. Roosevelt, in his anxiety to further that great measure, negotiated a treaty with Columbia, by which we were to be given the right to build the canal, and then Columbia rejected the treaty, and the residents of the Isthmus revolted—Panama revolted against Columbia and established a new government. Then very promptly—our Democratic friends said too promptly—but I do not think too promptly, because it was necessary to act in order that we should secure the right—we negotiated a treaty with Panama which gave us the right and power to build that canal. And now, under the Administration of Theodore Roosevelt, we have gone ahead and are building that canal.

Then, too, we had to meet the question of arid lands in the West, the reclamation of those lands. We had to meet a great many other questions: the pure food question, the meat inspection question, all of which enlarged the function of government, requiring the employment of many more civil servants, and extended the operations of the National Government, increasing the risk of efficiency in government. And yet I ask you, my fellow-citizens, whether there is a single stain upon the escutcheon of the Republican party under Theodore Roosevelt in meeting all these new problems? Not only that, but with respect to our foreign affairs, never in the history of the Nation has the standard of the United States been higher before the nations of the world than it is today.

My dear friends, you can recollect—I can distinctly—that four years ago we were told that if Theodore Roosevelt was put in power he would go around this country with a chip on his shoulder and involve us in war; that he was waiting for somebody to tread on the tail of his coat in order that he might have a fight. What was the result? It is not necessary for me to detail it, only to state that never before in the history of the world has a President of the United States and an administration, or any emperor or monarch, done more to preserve the peace of the world than has Theodore Roosevelt at the head of this Administration. Under those circumstances, gentlemen, I ask you what is the part of a wise people? Is it to select the agency which met all these new problems, has met them without scandal, without corruption, and with efficiency, which has carried the name of this nation to the head of nations, or to select a party which has opposed everything that was attempted to be done by the Administration in these matters? Gentlemen, I think there is but one answer to that question.

Now I come to another series of issues. The Dingley Bill was passed in 1897. Under that Dingley Bill we went ahead to a prosperity never before known in this country and indeed never before known in the world. The investment of capital and the expansion of business went on; wages were increased, and the standard of living of the wage-earners, of the business man and of the farmer was improved beyond precedent. But we found in the business world that we had expanded ourselves a little too far; that capital had become fixed in enterprises that did not make the return sufficient to induce further investment. Capital became frightened, and now we have had a halt in that prosperity. Capital is necessary, if we are going on and not embrace socialism; capital is necessary to be invested in order that business may go on, in order that wage-earners may be paid, in order that business men may earn an income, in order that farmers may have a market; and anything that is done to frighten invested capital, anything which leads invested capital to doubt the question whether a fair return will be paid, affects injuriously the wage-earner and the capitalist and the farmer. Now what I say is that the introduction into power of the Democratic party under its present leadership will create doubt of the future in the minds of the people, in the minds of those who will invest capital. These are not all millionaires. The capitalists of this country largely are the men who contribute to the savings banks, who contribute to make up in many small amounts the great fund that is subsequently invested in plants. Look at the list—the thirteen billions of deposits in the banks, and think how many millions of people contribute to that, and every one of them who contributes is a capitalist, and every one of them is affected by the question whether he is going to get his return on that little deposit he puts in. Now unless you assure capital a return, unless you can bring about that confidence in what is to be done, you may be certain that the return to prosperity which is now gradually assuming a definite form, will halt again, and I ask you in your hearts, whether you believe that the return of the Republican party to power under its leadership, or the return of the Democratic party under its leadership is the more likely to give confidence to the investment of capital in the future so that this prosperity that we have had may return to us again in full measure. In this great development of wealth, this magnificent stride onward and expansion of material prosperity there crept in abuses—abuses growing out of the greed and unscrupulous character of some of the prominent men engaged in business. They violated the Antitrust Law and they violated the Rebate Law, and the railroads extended to the larger shippers, the so-called "trusts," a means by which they could drive their competitors out of business by secret rebates. All this was revealed early in this Administration, and Mr. Roosevelt and the Republican party took hold with a determination to stamp it out. Now, I ask you, gentlemen, heart to heart, whether the action which Mr. Roosevelt took, whether the Rate Bill which the Republican party passed, whether the Pure Food Bill and the Meat Inspection Bill, and all those great measures of a Republican Congress were not an indication and a following of the moral awakening among the people in order to make the corporations understand that they must obey the law? Today rebates are abolished; the railroads have voluntarily acquiesced in that requirement; the trusts are engaged now in having lawyers consult the law to see how they may comply with it and avoid prosecution, and what we need now is a mere perfection of the machinery so as to keep and regulate the railroads and the trusts and keep them within the law. We don't wish to destroy these great organizations that have a large wage fund when they are prosperous and that add greatly to the prosperity of the country, but what we wish to do is to keep them within the law. That is the proposition of Mr. Roosevelt which he is responsible for before the country. That is what the Republican party stands for, and that is what the Republican party intends to do, if you give them an opportunity by your mandate to take the power.

But I am asked, "What is the relation of the Republican party to labor?" I want to make one statement first: that never in the history of this country has there been an Administration that has passed more measures directly in the interest of the laboring classes than the present Republican Administration.

Take the Employers' Liability Act. Of course, Congress is limited in what it can do to things that affect the Federal jurisdiction. Congress has passed a law now by which railroad men engaged in interstate railroads shall be put on a level with the corporation in dealing with it in respect to the damages that they sustain growing out of their employment. It used to be that when a man sued a railroad that was organized as a corporation and the railroad removed the suit to the Federal Court, he would find that the rule of law laid down in the Federal Court with reference to the defense of such suits was a great deal stricter against the employee than it would have been if tried in the State court under the Ohio law. In other words, that the fellow-servant rule was more strictly applied in the Federal courts under Supreme Court decision than it was in the State courts, and so too with the rule of contributory negligence, so that if there was the slightest evidence of any contributory negligence he forfeited his entire claim under the Employers' Liability Act. What is the law now? It is that it makes no difference whether a man is injured through the negligence of this co-employee or through the negligence of a superior officer of the company, the company is equally liable in both cases. So, too, if the man has been guilty of a slight contributory negligence, his recovery is a question that is left to the jury to apportion the damages as the expression is; that is, to reduce the damages to the ratio contributory negligence may bear to the negligence of the company or of the employee that led to the injury. This is a measure which, for a technicality, was thrown out by the Supreme Court, but has been re-passed in lawful form by the present Congress. Then there are all the safety appliance acts which I hope will tend to reduce the awful sacrifice of life and limb among the employees of the railroad companies. Then, too, there are other measures, the Government Employees' Compensation for Injuries Act, which requires interstate commerce employees to serve only a certain number of hours and forbids their service longer, and I would like to go on and mention other acts, the Fire Pan Act, and the act for the purpose of investigating the causes of those awful mine disasters that have killed so many people, without explanation of how the killing has been done. So I think if you will review the statutes, you will find that no Congress and no Administration has done as much to put the laboring man on a level in dealing with the company with reference to his employment as has the Republican Administration now which will end on the fourth of March next.

Now I come to the question of injunction. In the first place, I understand that my own personal attitude toward labor has been represented as a man who thinks and says that a dollar a day is enough for any man. Well, there is one short way of meeting that statement, and that is that it is a lie! I never said so, and I don't think that it argues intelligence in any man who believes the statement, for what under heaven would induce me or any one else to say so? In the second place, they say I am the "father of injunctions in labor cases." I have issued injunctions in labor cases, there is no doubt about that, and I have done it because the rights of the plaintiff entitled him to an injunction, and when I am on the Bench and enforcing the law, I enforce it, and I don't make any apologies for it. It has been my lot to sit in labor cases, to sit in antitrust cases. When I am a Judge of the Bench, in so far as I can, I decide cases according to the law and the facts, no matter whom it hurts, because I believe that to be my sworn duty. Now it has been my lot to lay down the rules with respect to the rights of labor in two or three cases, and I refer to those cases as a full statement of what I believe the rights of labor to be with reference to its employment. Labor has the right to unite in organizations for the purpose of looking after the united interest of labor in its controversy with capital, because if it did not unite and was not permitted to unite, then it would lie hopeless. Laborers have the right not only to unite but to contribute funds which in times when they wish to leave the employ of their employer when they do not like his terms, may support their fellow-members. They have the right to appoint officers who shall control their action if they choose. They have the right to invite all other laborers to unite with them in their controversy, and to withdraw if they choose from association with their employer. But they have not the right to injure their employer's property; they have not the right by what is called a "secondary boycott" to invite a third person into the controversy who wishes to keep out, by threatening a boycott with him, unless he assists them in the fight. In this fight between employer and the employee, or the united employees, they must fight it out between themselves, and they must not involve the rest of the community in it by a system of duress. This law, I believe, is a fair law, and being a fair law, when I was on the Bench I attempted to enforce it. With reference to injunctions, the question has been raised as to notice, whether an injunction ought to issue without notice. It is a fundamental principle of law that no man ought to be affected to his detriment in a judicial action without notice and hearing, and therefore, the ordinary rule was, in the United States Court, in the Judiciary Act years ago, that no temporary injunction could issue without notice; but there arose a few cases, as for instance where a man was in charge of property and was cutting down a tree, and the owner of the property wanted to save the tree, and unless he got his injunction served upon that man before the tree was cut down, he could not save the tree. He could get damages, but the damages did not compensate him at all for the tree. So in such a case an exception was introduced and it is a very rare case. Now, generally, I think in labor cases the character of the damage done by those workingmen who are lawless is not of that character which is like the cutting down of a tree, but the damage done arises from a constant nagging and a constant repetition, and generally in such cases there is no reason why notice should not be given before a restraining order shall be issued. So I have said, as President Roosevelt has said in the past, that it seemed to me that we might get back to the old practice according to the United States Court rules. But the Republican Convention felt that it was better not to go quite so far, but to put into operation by a statute carefully stating the law and specifying which injunctions might issue without notice, making them as rare as they ought to be. Under this Republican plank the statute may and should provide that an injunction issued without notice shall last only twenty-four or forty-eight hours, and then shall cease to be operative, unless the person enjoined, unless the defendant comes in and asks that the hearing be postponed. If the plaintiff who gets the injunction shall not come in for a hearing before the twenty-four or forty-eight hours, as the case may be, has expired, then the injunction expires by its own motion. That is the proposition under the Republican platform. Under the Democratic platform I do not know what the proposition is. It says nothing about notice. What the Democratic platform says is this: That injunctions ought not to issue in labor cases where they would not issue on other cases. Certainly they ought not. I do not know who ever said they ought to, but the impression sought to be given apparently is that they ought not to issue in labor cases at all, but that is not what the platform says. It says that they should not issue in labor cases if they do not issue in other cases.

It is said I introduced the injunction first in labor cases. That gives me too much credit for ingenuity and too great honor as an inventor of judicial proceedings. If you will examine authorities, you will find that there are a number of cases before I issued any injunction at all, and that I merely followed precedent in doing so. I am not apologizing for that. I am merely telling you the fact. What I believe, gentlemen, is that there ought to be no favored class in litigation at all, that a man who has property and a man who has labor to sell shall stand on an equality in court, and that every man shall be entitled to be protected by all the writs and remedies that the law affords, by an impartial judiciary, and that whether he be a laborer or business man or the owner of property, he is entitled to have his rights protected by all the writs that the law affords.

Now, gentlemen, this theory that if you weaken the courts by taking away the power of injunction in certain cases, you are going to help the workingman, is utterly unfounded. The person who is going to take advantage of the weakened power of the courts is the man who has wealth enough to enable him to employ acute lawyers to know what the technicalities are that he can take advantage of, and to know the weakness in the armor of the court that he can pierce, to know when he can escape the object of the law in the punishment of the really guilty person. The truth is, gentlemen, as we are now engaged in enforcing these great statutes which seek to punish and fine and imprison wealthy violators of the law, we begin to realize that the administration of our criminal law is quite defective, and that the great remedy that we need in this country is such facility and expedition in the trial of cases that the poor man shall not be at a disadvantage in court with the wealthy man. It is expedition that helps the poor man, because he cannot afford to have his case delayed.

And now, gentlemen, the final question is whether we shall have a jury trial in contempt proceedings. I say no, and I say no because we never have had a jury trial in such proceedings since the foundation of English and American jurisprudence, because if you introduced a jury trial between the enforcement of a court's order and the turning over to the man of what he is entitled to under that order, you only make another step in the delay of the court that denies justice. Now you know what the jury trial is. We have to have and ought to have jury trials in the cases fixed by the Constitution, but not in the enforcement of the court's order. This rule in the Democratic platform applies not only to preliminary injunction, not only to perpetual injunction, but to all other judgments of the court in which the defendant is required to do anything or not to do anything. Before that judgment of the court can be enforced, if the defendant chooses to hold himself aloof and ignore it, there must be a jury trial. Why, there must be a jury trial if a witness is subpœnaed, and the witness does not come into court, to determine whether the witness received the subpœna. If you summon a juryman and he does not come into court, you must have a jury to determine whether he got the summons. That is the effect of the provisions in the Democratic platform, and I say with great respect that such a provision strikes at the power of the courts. The civilization of our country depends on our making the courts more effective and in giving them power which shall enable them to do their business more quickly, which shall require them to do their work more quickly, so that justice may not drag on, one, two or three years. I am sure that the intelligent workingmen of this country, when they come to face the question whether they wish the tribunals for the administration of justice weakened to the point so that the people may laugh at it, or whether they wish them to be sustained, will forget their particular and especial interest in a class of cases and, like patriots as they are, will rise to the point of saying that the administration of the courts must be held high, that the power of the courts must be held up, so that they can enforce their own orders.

Now, gentlemen, I have talked to you as frankly as possible. I am here to show you that I have an interest and sympathy with the laboring man. I have attempted to lay down what his rights are, just as I did lay down what his rights are in judicial decisions, which I do not wish to discuss because, having been a Judge on the Bench, it is hardly proper for me to refer to those decisions and discuss them in detail. They speak for themselves. All I ask is that when the question is up for consideration, whether I have done such things as ought to condemn me and ought to condemn the party that I represent, you shall read the whole evidence and tell me whether they are not in accordance with the square deal and fairness in the administration of justice.

We really have no classes in this country in the old-country sense. We have a lot of millionaires and multi-millionaires, and we are apt to consider them a class. As a matter of fact, their children and their children's children may be without any money at all. The truth is that we are all in the same boat. When the country is prosperous we are all in a comfortable condition. When the country is not prosperous, wage-earners and business men and farmers are likely to suffer. It is true that the man who is ahead is the millionaire and he is able to live on without investing his capital, and the investment of capital is not nearly so necessary to him as it is to the wage-earner and the ordinary business man and the farmer. Therefore, what we are all interested in is the investment of capital by those who have it, and those who have it are not only millionaires but also the wage-earners and the saving and the thrifty among us who keep depositing the money in the savings banks and elsewhere, which is amassed in large funds and then used to create these plants to make a wage fund that brings the wages and creates business. Now then, our interest is all the same in having a fair deal to capital and a fair deal to the railroads and a fair deal to shippers and to the corporations engaged in industrial enterprises. Whenever they violate the law, then they are to be prosecuted to the end, and to be restrained by injunction; but when they keep within the law, then we are all happy if they are prosperous, because their prosperity adds to our prosperity. In other words, we are all in the same boat. It is not possible to have a condition of things by which wage-earners shall earn large wages, business men

40

shall earn large profits from their business, farmers large profits from the selling of their products, and the man who has the money, who is investing it, gets no profit at all. That is not possible. Some think it would be well if it could be so, but it cannot be that way, and therefore what we wish is fair treatment to all in order that the boat may sail on and give comfort and the enjoyment of happiness to all classes, wage-earners, business men, farmers and capitalists alike.

Now, gentlemen, there is only one issue between the wage-earner and the employer and that is as to the terms of employment, the size of the wages and length of the hours of the day, but that aside, the interest of the wage-earner is even greater than the interest of the capitalist in having capital earn a good reward, because when it does earn a good reward, you can count on the continued and progressive investment of capital, and that means a greater demand for labor; that means greater wages for labor, and it means therefore greater comfort and pleasure and enjoyment for all of us.

Now I have said something about the organization of labor. I am in favor of the organization of labor, because I believe that in that single controversy that arises between capital and labor, the organization of labor has enabled them to prevent the reduction of wages too quickly under a falling market. The employer naturally looks around for economies and finds that he can make some saving by reducing the wages. They can hold back and retard him in reducing the wages, then on a rising market, when profits are increasing, they can hasten the increase in wages. To that extent the organization of labor is most useful to the laboring people. More than that, it is most useful in facilitating the passage of such laws as we have seen in the last Congress—the Child Labor Law, the law with respect to the employers' liability, the compensation to government employees acts, the safety appliance laws and all those things move when the labor organizations get together and ask Congress to have them passed, and therefore it is wise that they should organize. That gives them great power and they must exercise that power within the law exactly as combinations of capital exercise their power within the law, and those of us, the middlemen between them, have the right to insist that both combinations shall keep within the law, and that we shall have courts with sufficient power and sufficient support from the public at large to see that both combinations do keep within the law.

4

Mr. Bryan's Claim to the Roosevelt Policies

Delivered at Sandusky, Ohio, September 8, 1908

Mr. Chairman, Ladies and Gentlemen
and Fellow-citizens of Ohio:

I feel like apologizing for calling you out in the middle of the day from your occupations which have a higher claim, possibly, than anything that those of us who stand upon the stage can say to you. But it is not likely that I am going to have an opportunity of coming to Sandusky again during the campaign, and I seize this occasion, therefore, to say something in reference to one of the issues that are presented. Before coming to that, however, I would like to take up the suggestion of the last speaker with reference to the present condition of business and the present condition with respect to industrial matters.

Last year there was a financial panic and there has followed it a financial depression. For twelve years we had been going on at such a speed of expansion that we got too far spread out. Projects in which money had been invested did not pay and we had, therefore, what follows from action and reaction in the history of all countries—a lack of confidence on the part of those who invest capital, who declined to continue to invest in order that the plants which had been created might go on and continue the industries as they had been conducted for the last four or five years. Confidence is a plant of slow growth, and the result was that industries stopped. There became a great many unemployed, and no one would advance money. Now all of us, whether we are wage-earners, professional men, farmers or business men, are in one boat with respect to prosperity. We are all interested in having the men who have money, whether that money comes from the savings banks or the laborer, from the day-worker or the business man, or whether it comes from the pocket of the multi-millionaire, or the man of moderate means, we are all interested that those who invest money shall continue to invest it, and we all know that they will not invest it unless they are going to have a fair profit out of it. Therefore, it is to the interest of all of us that capital, whether it is in the pocket of the workingman who may deposit it in the savings bank, or in the pocket of the millionaire, that we should believe that when we invest it it is going to bring a fair return. In other words, confidence in the business future of the country is necessary if we are to have a return of prosperity.

I will not go into a discussion of reasons, but I state this proposition, and I state it to men who know it in their hearts, to men and women—for we want the influence of the women in this campaign—we know that the election of the Democratic party, with Mr. Bryan in the Presidency, is a menace to the confidence of the business community in the future. I am not going to state the reason but I'll state the fact, and that fact, therefore, ought to influence all who desire the unemployed to become employed, who desire business to become good, who desire that we shall have a return of the prosperity that we enjoyed for the last twelve years—will influence all of them to vote against the party and the leadership that does constitute a menace to our future prosperity.

I am going to take up another phase of the campaign. Mr. Bryan says that he is not only the heir of Theodore Roosevelt, with respect to the policies which Theodore Roosevelt has made honored the country through, but that he is also the parent of those policies. So that in default of an heir (because he says I am not an heir) as parent under the Ohio statutes or common law, he would take as heir by ascent. Now it is well to investigate that statement. Let us see what the Roosevelt policies are. Let us see what has been done by Mr. Roosevelt under those policies. Let us

43

see what Mr. Bryan proposes to do, and I submit that if Mr. Bryan proposes remedies and policies which the man whose name is attached to those policies does not recognize but condemns, we show that this claim of heirship has no foundation whatever. One of the things that is wise in this campaign and, indeed, in any campaign, is to get at the facts, to know what it is we are talking about. Now what are the Roosevelt policies? First, why was it necessary that there should be such policies? In twelve years of the marvelous business expansion that we had, from 1896 down to 1907, there necessarily crept in abuses growing out of the greed and unscrupulous character of some of the men engaged in carrying on that expansive prosperity. Human nature is the same yesterday, today and tomorrow, and there were men who took advantage of the situation and created evils and were unscrupulous in the methods which they pursued. Now, they were men who were governed by a desire for success, by a greed of financial power, and the principle that Mr. Roosevelt laid down was this: That in so far as those men violated the law, moral or statutory, they ought to be restrained, and in so far as the moral law was not covered by the statutes, that statutes ought to be created to cover it, so that the men who were wealthy and powerful should be subjected to the law and its punishment, its penalties, exactly as the men without influence and without means. Those are the Roosevelt policies as applied to the evils growing out of this period of expansion of twelve years.

Now, what were those evils? The evil was, speaking technically, the violation of the Antitrust Law in interstate commerce. It was the aggregation of wealth in plants so great the owners of it were able, by cunningly devised means, to stifle competition, to control prices of goods and shove them up above what the cost of production would justify. We admit—everybody with any reason admits—that the combination of capital is absolutely essential so that we should progress. It is just exactly the same as the combination of the parts of a machine in order that we may make things more easily than we make things by hand, and more cheaply. It inures to the benefit of the public by reducing the price of a product. And so the combination of capital in creating these large plants reduces the cost of production to the public, but if the men who unite those plants and create those combinations, though they reduce the cost of production, at the same time are able by those methods to maintain the prices, then they are deriving all the benefits and the public is deriving none. Now, it is that immoral and illegal use of combination toward which Mr. Roosevelt is directing his attention.

What were the means by which these combinations were able to suppress competition? The chief, the greatest one, was by obtaining from railroads secret rebates and unlawful discrimination in favor of those large combinations and to the disadvantage of the smaller competitors of those combinations. When you consider the enormous output of one of those great combinations you can see that the reduction of a cent a ton would be a very heavy profit or a very heavy advantage in favor of a great combination and against the smaller competitor. These secret rebates greatly exceeded a cent a ton, and I do not hesitate to say that the chief method by which these great illegal monopolies and trusts were fostered and maintained, was through the obtaining from the railroads of this secret discrimination in their favor. So, Mr. Roosevelt said that the first thing we have got to do (the Antitrust Law having been passed in 1890, as I shall hereafter point out) is to take hold of the railroads in such a way as to abolish this unlawful discrimination and these unlawful rebates. And so he did. Before he was elected, in the term succeeding Mr. McKinley, Congress passed what was called the Elkins Bill against rebates, and subsequently, in the first two years of his second term, they passed what was called the Rate Bill. Those two bills placed the railroads under the close supervision of the Government and made their proceedings so public, or at least, so well known to the Government officers, as to make it well-nigh impossible for them to continue the system of rebates. But the railroads did not wait. They became themselves convinced that it was necessary in order to save themselves from radical measures, in order that their business might again become honest, in order that they might conduct the business within the law, that this whole system should be abandoned, and it was abandoned and rebates today substantially have been abolished and that means by which unlawful combinations can be built up has been wiped out.

But let us examine some of the other methods. The Antitrust Law was passed in 1890. It was passed by a Republican Congress, the first Congress under Mr. Harrison. A Democratic Congress—I do not like to be hard on my Democratic friends but the truth in history has to be stated—a Democratic Congress had been in power or a Democratic house had been elected and had sat on this trust question for a full two years with a great committee that was going to solve the whole question. And what did they do? They took volumes of testimony so thick that it would discourage anyone from reading it, and then they resolved at the end of the last session, just before a Republican Congress was coming in, that they would make no recommendation with respect to the trusts and the evil of trusts and the method of suppressing them, because there was such a difference of opinion in the committee that they could not make any recommendation, and so they turned it all over to the next Republican Congress that came in.

Now, what follows? And this is perfectly typical of the difference between the two parties. Mr. Bryan says that the trusts control the Republican party, therefore, what can we hope from the Republican party, built up by trusts, or the tariff and otherwise? What does history show? It shows that the Democratic party when it had the power said: "We cannot agree as to a method." And the Republicans passed the only law that has been put on the statute books to suppress trusts, to wit: in 1890 the Sherman Antitrust Law, and that is the law that Theodore Roosevelt has been enforcing in the last seven years in a way that it had never been enforced before. Let us examine that Antitrust Law, because I like to get down to the statutes and words and facts. I am not an orator. I cannot dwell in the fountains of the cerulean blue. I have got to take facts. What are they?

The first section of the Antitrust Law is against combination in restraint of trade, the second section denounces illegal monopolies, and the two sections classify those entities which have been guilty of violating the law. Under the first, which is rather the easiest to deal with, one corporation here, another corporation there, another corporation there and a fourth corporation here, would unite together, not their whole business, but they would just enter into an agreement by which they would maintain prices, would restrict output and would divide between them what the profits were. That is, they would keep up the prices by this agreement and controlling as they did a large part of the output, they were able to carry out their conspiracy against the freedom of trade.

Well, several questions arose. The first one was whether an industrial corporation that gathered together manufacturing plants in various States could be restrained from buying those plants on the ground that it was violating the Antitrust Law. The Supreme Court of the United States said it could not. That was what was known as the "sugar trust case." It is said the mere purchase of plants was a question for State control and not for National control. And so, after that decision, Mr. Olney, the Attorney-general of Mr. Cleveland, gave it as his opinion that the Federal Government was without power to do anything to suppress this evil.

But they went ahead with other cases and finally they got a case like this, in which perhaps fifteen or twenty cast-iron pipe companies united together and distributed the business through the different territories, agreed on prices that they were to charge, divided up the business, and then a stenographer of the president or the manager of the whole concern, not getting what he thought he ought to out of this conspiracy, betrayed the combination and the stenographic notes were opened, the case was prosecuted, an injunction was issued, the case came before the court, and it was held that as it showed a conspiracy to control interstate commerce between the States in cast iron pipe, the Federal Government had the right to impose a penalty for that kind of thing, that it was within the function of the United States courts to punish it under the criminal law of the United States, and that it was within the function of the Government to provide that an injunction might issue to prevent the carrying on of such a conspiracy.

That was what was known as the Addyston pipe case that went from the Circuit Court of Appeals to the Supreme Court and was upheld. That case, I think, is probably the most important case in determining what the power of a national government is in respect to them. But then, just as soon as they began to direct their attention to corporations, then the corporations united in one corporation and they said: "We have not made any agreement with anybody; we are a legal entity, recognized by law; we just agree with ourselves and that agreement certainly is not in violation of law." But what they were attempting to do was to monopolize the business in particular lines and the question was whether they were not using illegal methods to accomplish that purpose.

Now, what are those illegal methods? They consist generally in the use of some kind of duress growing out of the fact that they are able to control a large part of the plants engaged in the business. For instance, they will make a contract with their customers excluding the patronage of their customers with anybody else, saying: "We will sell you goods at a certain price and we will give you a rebate on those goods if you don't patronize our competitors." Or they go into one part of the country where they have a small competitor and they will undersell him so as to drive him out of business, in the meantime charging exorbitant prices in other parts of the country. Those are badges of duress, badges of fraud, and it is that character of things that makes the aggregation of capital for the purpose of monopoly illegal. That it is a monopoly and therefore illegal appears by reason of these methods thus pursued, because you must bear in mind that the mere aggregation of capital for economic purposes—to wit: to reduce the cost of production—is not illegal. It is the use of a great amount of aggregate plant not for the purpose of reducing the cost of production but for the purpose of driving others out of business by the methods that I have detailed, that is a violation of the statutes. What we want is the large plants; we need them, they give an enormous wage fund, they reduce the cost of production, they make a large part of the prosperity of the country and we don't want to drive those men out of business, providing they keep within the laws.

Now, Mr. Roosevelt went ahead, as I have said, and instigated more prosecutions—and he is continuing to do so today—than in all administrations which have preceded him. There came early in this Administration a revelation with respect to the extent to which these illegal monopolies had taken their hold on business and there was an awakening of the conscience of the people, and Mr. Roosevelt interpreted that conscience and put into force what the people with their aroused conscience demanded, and that is the reason why they call those policies the Roosevelt policies.

Now what remains to be done? I believe that a tremendous step forward has been made in restricting these evils, that the greatest instrumentality by which these trusts may have been built up—these illegal trusts—has been the rebates of the railroads, and those are utterly abolished. Then, too, the prosecutions of these great companies have made them consult lawyers, have made them feel the fear of penalty in their hearts and they are keeping on generally within the law.

Now, what is it we need ? What we need is to increase the machinery of government, to increase the supervision of these combinations that have the temptation to violate the law so that under the eye of government agents it can be seen easily whether they are keeping within the law and

that the departments at Washington shall have assistance enough and organization enough so that these prosecutions can be carried on with great
rapidity, that when a man is charged with violating the law he can find out
quickly what the law is and how far he can go, how far legitimate business
methods will go and then we shall have a condition where he will keep
within the law and not destroy the business that is necessary to continue
the prosperity of the country.

If I am elected I propose to devote all the ability that is in me to the
constructive work of suggesting to Congress a means by which the Roosevelt policies shall be clinched, but that is to be done, not with a turn of the
hand, not, as Governor Harris said at Youngstown, by a magician's wand;
it is to be done by men who understand the operation of the statutes, who
know what the law means, who understand its practical workings and with
a consciousness that reforms of this kind are not to be brought about by
the mere passage of a statute, but also by its earnest enforcement, step by
step, until the public and those who are likely to violate it, shall understand
that the penalty will be theirs if they do.

Let us see what Mr. Bryan's methods are, in order to know whether
this heirship of Mr. Roosevelt's, that he desires, has any foundation whatever. He proposes, first, to take off the duty on every article which is manufactured by trusts and controlled by them. Well, now let us see what Mr.
Roosevelt thinks about that. He has had four years and if you will examine
his letter of acceptance four years ago you will find he took up that proposed remedy and said it was not only utterly impracticable but it was
utterly unjust. He said it was not only impracticable because you cannot
tell who is to determine what is a trust controlled article and what is not
and, on the other hand, the remedy means the destruction not only of
the illegal trusts but it means the destruction of every honest and lawful
competitor of that trust, because the business of the one is just as dependent upon a protective tariff as the business of the other, and, therefore,
you are going to involve in that remedy the destruction of the innocent
with the guilty.

So, too, it is proposed to change from the protective tariff to the revenue tariff in order to avoid trusts. Well, they have trusts in countries that
never had a revenue tariff. Therefore, while it may be true that a protected
industry might be more easily monopolized than one that is not protected,

because you have to include the whole, the question which we have to decide is whether it is not better to attack the evil itself than to sacrifice all our industries dependent upon a protective system, in order to stamp out evils in a comparatively few of them. Now, that, I say, is the difference between Mr. Roosevelt and Mr. Bryan, and when Mr. Bryan says that he is the heir of the Roosevelt policies, he means that he is going to carry on an attack on the evils which Mr. Roosevelt directed his attention against, and against which he has made most substantial progress, by remedies which are disapproved by Mr. Roosevelt and remedies which instead of commending themselves to the people, will involve us all in disaster, because it will be punishing the innocent with the guilty.

I have talked as far as I have a right to hold your attention today. I have taken up merely the Roosevelt policies. There is one more important question which, if I am elected, I expect to devote as much time to as possible to bring about a proper solution of, and that is the question of the overissue of the stocks and bonds of interstate railways, and that is part of the Roosevelt policies and it becomes a part in this wise: that this overissue of bonds and stocks upon the real value of the railroads puts in the power of the monopolies a means of getting stocks and bonds which they sell on the market and then buy other railroads. The history of the Chicago & Alton and other railways will show that that was the way by which the one man in control of the first company concentrated power and control over many other companies, and so it produces a concentration and control of railways that does not make for the public good.

The question is whether the Federal Government can pass a law effecting that purpose, because interstate railways though they may be doing an interstate commerce business and running across State lines, yet they are State corporations. The question is whether you can have a Federal government interfering with the bonds and stocks of State corporations. My judgment is that it is possible to do so with respect to interstate railways, on the theory that the overissue of stocks and bonds of such a railway is so likely to interfere with the efficient operation of that railway for the public benefit, that the United States may step in and say, "Here, you must not weigh down your railroad and prevent its improvement by proper construction and re-construction, by issuing obligations which will consume your entire income in paying the interest on those obligations, and not using that income for the construction and proper repair of your railways, and the efficient discharge of your duty as an interstate common carrier." This is cited in the Republican platform as one of the measures that are needed to carry on the work that Mr. Roosevelt has so well begun and carried on to such an encouraging point of progress.

There are other measures to which I could refer, but I have gone over this matter of the Roosevelt policies in order to point out to you that Mr. Bryan has no more right to say that he is the heir of the Roosevelt policies, in view of what he proposes to do if he gets into power, considering Mr. Roosevelt's own view as to what ought to be done, than the Tichborne claimant had to the Tichborne estates. You will remember that Mr. Arthur Orton appeared as the Tichborne heir and the result was very disastrous to him personally before he got through, for while he pointed out a great many reasons why he was the heir, it was found after a discussion of all those reasons, and the introduction of evidence, that he was only a distant friend of the real heir.

Ladies and gentlemen, I thank you for your attention. I apologize for taking up your time at this time of the day, but I had no other time in which I could direct my remarks.

5

The Future of the Negro

Delivered at Allen Temple, Cincinnati, Ohio, September 15, 1908

My Friends:

I am glad to meet this audience in Allen Temple. I have been here before, and I have long known members of this congregation. One of the prominent pillars of the church, James A. S. Clark, was for a long time a client of my father and of me. I am glad to meet the representatives of the African Methodist Episcopal Church, because I know that they exercise a wide influence among the colored peoples and especially among those of their church.

I am not here tonight to talk politics. At the invitation of the presiding elder I am here to give you greeting and to express my sympathy with your race in the struggle that it is making for better things. It is a sympathy which I have had from the time I was a small boy, for I inherited it from my father, Alphonso Taft, than whom the colored race never had a better friend.

My interest in the race and the problems that its progress presents has been stimulated by my experience in the Philippines, for there I had to deal with a brown race that, like the colored race in this country, is engaged

cheer—the future is brighter for him and is more in his hands than ever. While the Negro is the ward of the nation, in the sense that the nation brought him here against his will, and must now deal with the problems that his presence presents and solve them justly, fairly and charitably, he is not thereby relieved from the burden of responsibility that he must assume to win his way in the community by industry and thrift, to a place in which he becomes too valuable a part of society for his depreciators to ignore his rights and well-earned position.

I thank you for the opportunity of meeting you and of expressing my sympathy with the work which you are all doing, and my hope of continued progress on the part of your people toward higher things.

6

In Defense of the Philippine Policy

Addressed to the Citizens of Norwood, Ohio, at the Sinton Hotel, September 19, 1908

My Friends from Norwood:

I am very much obliged to you for coming to greet me tonight. You are my neighbors, and I am glad to talk to you. I have selected for a subject for discussion one very near to my heart, and that is the Philippine Islands. They are an issue in this campaign.

The Democratic party has declared in its platform that as soon as a stable government is established in the Islands we should leave them. A stable government is established, so that this is equivalent to a resolution in favor of immediate withdrawal. The Republican party has declared in favor of continuing its present policy which is that of continuing a government in which popular control by the Filipinos is being from time to time enlarged, in which every effort is being made to give the people of the Islands education and also experience in self-government, in order that ultimately the time may come, in one generation or two, when it will be safe for the people of the Islands to give them complete control over the Government.

When the Spanish War ended, and we were in potential control of the

Archipelago, there was only one of three courses for us to pursue: either to turn the islands back to Spain, to turn them over to Aguinaldo and his army, or to take them under our sovereignty. The first course would have been unfair to the Filipinos, who with us engaged in a war to drive Spain out of the islands, and as allies they were entitled to an arrangement which should not bring them again within the control of Spain. We could not turn the islands over to Aguinaldo, because he had attempted to govern them for eight or nine months under our observation, and the Government had miserably failed. The tyranny and corruption of it quite exceeded that of the Spanish Government, of which so much complaint was made by the Filipinos. There was nothing for us to do, therefore, but to assume responsibility ourselves, take over the Government and to enter upon the altruistic policy of educating the people in every way possible, giving them practice in governing themselves, so that step by step they might be advanced toward the ideal of a self-governing people.

The people were suspicious and did not believe in the announcement of the McKinley policy of attraction, and a war of insurrection against the United States was begun by Aguinaldo and his supporters which it became necessary, for the tranquillity of the Government, for the United States to put down. An army was raised and the war was put down. Tranquillity was restored by the use of the army and also by the carrying out of the policy of attraction by establishing autonomy in the municipalities, partial autonomy in the provinces and by giving Filipinos representatives in the Commission conducting the central government. This was done before the insurrection was ended, and was largely the cause of its complete cessation.

In adopting this policy Mr. McKinley met the bitter opposition of the leaders of the Democratic party, and most prominent among them was Mr. Bryan. In 1900, in the first presidential campaign after the close of the Spanish war, Mr. Bryan announced that the paramount issue was anti-imperialism. He and those who supported him in that campaign, and who had indicated their policy even before the campaign came on, condemned the course of McKinley with so much vehemence as to convince the Filipinos that it was wise for them to continue in open insurrection, and Mr. Bryan and his followers were responsible for the cost and suffering and loss of life on both sides which arose during the unnecessary year of war. Since

1900 we have been engaged, first, in restoring tranquillity; second, in maintaining justice; third, in spreading education; fourth, in the construction of public improvements in the Islands; fifth, in the settlement of the church questions growing out of the transfer from a government in which the Church and State were inextricably united to one in which they must be completely separate; sixth, in promoting the hygiene of the Islands by the establishment of efficient quarantine and a general health department throughout the Archipelago.

We supplemented the army by the establishment of an Island constabulary force of natives, officered by Americans in part, which reached in number about 5,000, and which was distributed through the various provinces of the Islands in such a way as to assist the native governors elected to preside over the destinies of their provinces, to preserve peace and suppress ladronism.

We established a system of courts of first instance with jurisdiction embracing the entire Archipelago, together with a Supreme Court. We filled the court partly with Filipinos and partly with Americans, and the administration of justice has been fearless and effective. Some poor appointments have been made, but generally the system has worked well.

Ninety percent of the people of the Philippine Islands are densely ignorant. It is this state of ignorance which unfits them for popular self-government. Education is their first need. We sent for one thousand American school-teachers to begin the work. We decided to teach the youth of the Islands English, because it is the language of free institutions; it is the language which most of the people desire their children to learn; it is the business language of the Orient, and it is the language of the country which is assisting the Filipinos to their feet. By earnest effort, the one thousand teachers brought over have taught English to six or seven thousand Filipino teachers, and they in turn are carrying on the primary schools of the Islands, under the supervision of American superintendents. There are today in the schools of the Islands upward of 500,000 children reading, writing and reciting in English. The system is not extensive enough, but we are limited by our means. If the United States were to give us three or four millions of dollars a year, we could use it economically and carry on a school system which would probably make room for all the youth of school age in the Islands.

We have completed the construction of a harbor at Manila, at a cost of some $4,000,000, which makes Manila one of the best harbors in the Orient, and we are engaged in similar work at Iloilo and Cebu. Many wagon roads have been constructed in the Islands, and the system is now being worked out by which the people shall have a motive for taking care of the roads. This problem is most difficult in a place like the Philippines, where the rains are so heavy in the wet season as to wash out any known material in the roads.

Among the roads in the Islands which were constructed was the Benguet road. This road led from the lowlands up the gorge of the Bued River some twenty odd miles, and involved us in a cost of $2,000,000. Had we known in advance that the cost would have been so great we never should have undertaken the task, but now that it is done it has brought about such a change in the Islands that the improvement is worth all it cost. The road leads from the lowlands to a rolling plateau 5,500 feet high, in which the temperature varies within the limits of 40 degrees and 80 degrees Fahrenheit. With the exception of the rainy month of August the climate in Benguet is as fine as any in the world. The plateau is covered with pine trees and grass, and makes a most delightful summer climate. Criticism was at first heard that this road was built merely for the purpose of enabling American officials to get away in the summer, but lots have been sold from the Government reservation under a law providing for advertisement and many Filipinos have bought; all the churches have bought, and most of them are establishing houses to which they can send persons for a month or two to recuperate. Schools and sanatoriums are being established, and it is the great health resort of the Archipelago. It is hardly too much to say that Benguet has become as popular and as useful among the Filipinos as among the Americans. There is every reason to expect that the National Assembly will meet there next year.

The greatest need in the material development of the Islands is the construction of railways. Under the organic act of 1902, Congress gave us authority to grant railway franchises, but try as we would, we were not able to enlist capitalists in the enterprise except in the construction of two small lines, branches of the old road. In 1905, Congress passed a law enabling us to guarantee the interest on the bonds of any new railway to the extent of 4 percent for thirty years, the amounts paid to be a second lien on the railroad payable after thirty years. By this means we have secured the construction of 100 miles of railroad in each of the three leading islands of Negros, Cebu and Panay. In Luzon, we secured the construction of 400 miles of additional railway without any guaranty. It was secured in this wise: The Manila and Dagupan road had been built under a Spanish franchise creating a partnership in the railroad between the Government and the company and having among its many terms a guaranty of a fixed income to the company during the life of the franchise for eighty-eight years. Under the advice of the Attorney-general of the United States that the provisions of the charter, and especially the guaranty, were not binding on the United States, the military government before I became Governor had declined to pay the income when demanded, and repudiated the obligations of the charter. This left the franchise in a most indeterminate condition. In subsequent negotiation we secured a contract with the company to construct 400 additional miles in Luzon under a perpetual franchise, by bringing the old railroad under the same franchise. All the railroad franchises authorized by the present government in the Philippines are perpetual just as they are in this country. They all contain the provision, however, that they are subject to amendment or repeal by Congress. The arrangement made was greatly for the public benefit.

This is the part of my record in the Philippines to which I suppose Mr. Bryan means to call my attention. He speaks of the Benguet railroad franchise. There is no Benguet railroad. I wish there was. I presume he refers to this Manila and Dagupan railroad franchise. It was fully described in an elaborate report I made to Congress in 1906. It was approved by the President and the Cabinet after full consideration. Mr. Bryan is the first person, so far as I know, to question its wisdom or propriety.

Next we bought the friars' lands and paid $7,000,000 for them. This was done to save a new insurrection by the 60,000 tenants on the land who refused to pay rent to the friars. The friars had good title to the lands, but they had become unpopular with the people and the tenants refused to recognize their title, claiming that Aguinaldo's government had passed a law nationalizing these lands and that therefore they would not recognize the friars as their lawful owners. The purchase rid the Government of the necessity of enforcing at the instance of the friars judgments in the courts for the ejection of 60,000 tenants, and thus averted a new war. And not only in the matter of the friars' lands but in the matter of many charitable trusts, we have effected a compromise by which the church takes over some charitable trusts, and we take over others. All the church questions are settled, well settled and fairly settled. Meantime the influence for good of the Catholic Church in the Philippines has been increased by the substitution of an American hierarchy for the Spanish hierarchy. Episcopal, Methodist, Presbyterian and Baptist churches have been established there, and a great improvement has come over the Islands with respect to religion and morality, after the demoralization of four years' war and desolation.

We have organized a comprehensive health department, very necessary in a country so much exposed to infectious diseases as the Philippines are. The diseases are not confined to human beings, but the rhinderpest and the surra have destroyed 75 percent of the cattle and 50 percent of the horses. We have had to resist an epidemic of plague and an epidemic of cholera, and to be constantly working to suppress the cattle and horse diseases that I have mentioned.

We first gave the Filipinos autonomy in their municipal governments, so that those eligible to vote were limited to persons who could read and write Spanish, read and write English, or who paid a tax of $7.50 a year, or who had formerly filled office in municipalities. Secondly, we gave partial autonomy in the provinces by providing for the election of a Governor, and third we gave representation in the legislative body, the Commission, to three Filipinos out of eight. Then we increased the autonomous character of the provincial governments by providing for the election of two out of three of the controlling provincial board, and leaving only the provincial treasurer to be appointed by the central government. Under the act of Congress for framing the government of the Philippines, provision was made for a National Assembly to be selected in districts distributed through the Christian part of the Philippine Islands by the voters under the rules above stated. This National Assembly was established last year, and while a majority of them are so-called "Independistas" and favor in their party immediate independence, they have coöperated with the Government in such a way as to show that the Assembly was a step forward and a good thing both for the purpose of following public opinion and by practically instructing the people of the Philippines in self-government.

In an interview I said that even the Independistas—that is, those in favor of immediate independence in the Islands—prefer Republican victory to Mr. Bryan's promises. Mr. Bryan now responds with a cable from Alberto Barretto denying this on behalf of certain authorities in the Independista party. I relied for my statement on a conversation I had last month with Señor Quezon, who is the leader of the Independistas in the National Assembly, in which he told me that although the Independistas liked Mr. Bryan's platform they preferred my election as a friend of the Filipino to Mr. Bryan's promises. This statement Señor Quezon subsequently repeated in a published interview. There is evidently a difference of opinion among the Independistas.

The helpful work of the schools and churches in the Islands is carried on apace. The spirit of Christian emulation has been infused into the community among the churches, and with the spread of education there is no reason why the progress already made may not continue. I speak of the churches in the Philippines from the standpoint of one interested especially in the governmental and political welfare of the Islands. The Filipino people are naturally a religious people, and therefore their churches are to be made a most efficient instrumentality in their uplifting, and the wise legislator and the wise statesman in their interest cannot but encourage all church environment. My conviction upon the Philippine question is that we are in the Islands for an altruistic purpose; that the fortune of war and fate and Providence sent us to the Philippines; that the Islands came into our hands in such a way that we were, under the international obligation, forced to keep peace in the Islands, and to see to it that foreign interests there did not suffer; that the delivery from the Spanish power at our instance thrust the Islands, in so far as their people were concerned, upon this country, and made it our duty to look after the welfare of all the people, and especially the welfare of the 90 percent of densely ignorant who did not know and could not know what their interests were; that to turn them over to Aguinaldo and his generals for government, as shown by the experiment actually tried, was to turn the Islands over to chaos and a condition of continual warfare between the factions in the Islands which would lay waste the Islands and retard them many decades in their growth. As a great rich nation in the family of nations, whenever fate shall thrust a poor, unfortunate people upon our hands, it is our duty, exactly as it is the duty of the fortunate in a community, to aid the unfortunate, and we cannot escape by international agreements or otherwise the direct responsibility that we now have to the Filipino people.

In my judgment, it would be a cowardly policy for us to give up our work in the Philippines when so much remains to be done in order to secure the permanent effect of our policy. By making free trade between the Islands and the United States, as recommended by the Republican platform, we shall bring advantage to both countries, and we shall see a prosperity in the Islands that will make their trade worth having. I do not advocate this policy merely to benefit the United States. I am more interested in it really for the benefit of the Philippines, because the United States is such a great prosperous country that it can afford to get along without additional Philippine trade. Nevertheless, the result of our altruistic policy, the result of our dealing with the Philippines for the benefit of the Filipinos only, in the end will turn out to be the best possible course for the betterment of our American trade with the Islands.

Mr. Bryan says that we have adopted his policy in the Philippines; that he has desired to give the Philippines independence and that we propose to give them independence. Let us examine the facts in respect to this statement of Mr. Bryan and see whether he fairly states the whole truth.

Mr. Bryan's method of giving them independence was to release them at once, immediately after the Treaty of Paris, and let them make the best way they could, through bloody faction and chaos, to decent self-government. And his further method was to interfere as much as possible, by agitation in this country and vehement denunciation of our policy, with the efforts which we were making to bring tranquillity and peace to the Islands. We have always contended that the immediate independence which Mr. Bryan wishes to give the Philippines would result in the utmost misery to the inhabitants of the Islands. We thought that the best method of procedure was to take over the Islands, to give them a good government, to educate the ignorant, to practise the people in partial self-government until they should be fit to take over the government themselves, and then, if they desired it, to turn it over to them. We felt and still feel that it would be unwise definitely to promise independence to the Filipinos for the reason that it encourages constant agitation and a construction of the promise to mean independence in the near future, whereas there is the strongest probability that the people of the Islands will not be fit for complete self-government under two generations, and when they are, it is further probable that, rather than have a complete separation from the United States and independence, they will prefer to enjoy the benefit of an association with the United States like that which Australia or Canada has with Great Britain.

I submit there is not the slightest resemblance between our policy and that which Mr. Bryan proposes. It is true that eight years of our rule in the Philippines have produced tranquillity and brought about a good government of the Islands, and that the people are as happy as they could be under untoward conditions arising from natural causes, and therefore, that although Mr. Bryan in 1900 declared that the paramount issue was that of anti-imperialism, he has with his accustomed dexterity and liberality in the matter of paramount issues, passed from anti-imperialism to something which he regards as more attractive to the people.

The truth is that our treatment of the Philippines, our recognition of the rights of the people there, our attempt to teach them practical self-government, our exaltation of the individual, have had an excellent effect throughout the Orient. It is felt in China; it is felt in India. We are pioneers in spreading the Western civilization in the East. Our course in the Philippines has been denounced by Mr. Bryan and the Democratic party as a departure from the principles of the Declaration of Independence and with humiliation to the real lovers of liberty in this country. Mr. Bryan in 1900 went so far as to say that unless he were elected on the issue of anti-imperialism and the course of Mr. McKinley rebuked, we might as well hold no more Fourth of July celebrations for real patriotism would have departed from among us. Instead of this, by our course in the Archipelago we have spread liberty—not suppressed it. What our forefathers in the Declaration of Independence meant by liberty was liberty recommended by law, liberty with peace and tranquillity; liberty where the rights of the individual were respected—not license, not chaos, not freedom to cut each others' throats, but liberty under wise and enlightened government, of protected right to pursue happiness; the impartial administration of justice; the education of the people, and teaching them what their rights are. How can liberty be given to a people so dense in ignorance that they don't understand what liberty is? They must be taught. Our real wards are not the really educated wealthy people of the Philippines, numbering but 5 or 10 percent of the population; they are the ignorant 90 percent, and we shall not discharge our plighted duty to them until we can be sure that the government which is to be established over them will secure to them their rights and not maintain them in a permanent state of darkest ignorance. Hence I say, my fellow-citizens and neighbors, that one of the great reasons for keeping Mr. Bryan out of the Presidency and his party out of the control of Congress is that they are pledged to abandon the Islands, to adopt the policy of scuttle, to rid this Government of the burden which it has assumed with respect to this people and to halt the spread of civilization in that part of the Orient.

7

The Republican Party: What It Has Done

Delivered before the National League of Republican Clubs, at the Music
Hall, Cincinnati, Ohio, September 22, 1908

Gentlemen of the National League of Republican Clubs:

Your enthusiasm and your numbers are a good augury of the result in the present election. You are here because you believe in the Republican party; because you believe that it keeps its promises; because you believe the party is one that has cohesive power enough and governmental experience and statesmanship enough to do things; because you believe that it has in it the moral force to resist selfish influences that attempt to turn it from its purpose, and to pursue a course consistent with the public interest.

The party has been in power for eleven years just past and for forty years in the last forty-eight years. The record of its achievements, however, is so long that in a single speech, and in the time in which I can properly allot myself here, there is really no opportunity to go back to the days of Lincoln and Grant and Hayes and Garfield and Arthur and Harrison, although that period was rich in arduous deeds done by the party.

Confining ourselves to the last twelve years, we find a marvelous list of accomplishments. In the first place, through the instrumentality of the party, we defeated free silver, maintaining the gold standard, and stamped on repudiation. In the second place, in the interest of the freedom of Cuba, we fought the Spanish War, and brought it in a short but eventful struggle to glorious victory. In the next place, we accepted the responsibilities and the consequences of that war, and took over, under our care, not only Cuba but Porto Rico and the Philippines. The situation was one of the greatest difficulty. We encountered in the policies pursued the bitter opposition of the Democratic party, and this produced an embarrassment most costly both in life and blood. We passed the Dingley Tariff Bill, and substituted it for the Gorman-Wilson Bill which had laid waste the industries of this country and had stopped the fires and the wheels of trade and had thrown out of employment a greater percentage of the wage-earners than ever before in the history of the world; and by the establishment of our currency on a sound, honest basis, and the re-adoption of the protective system, we brought about a prosperity which has never been exceeded in the history of this country or any other. Negotiations had been pending and efforts had been making for years and years looking to the construction of the Panama Canal that might unite the two oceans, that might double the efficiency of our Navy, and that might add greatly to the cause of civilization and the commerce of the world. Pressing this question to a conclusion with Colombia resulted in a revolution in Panama, the establishment of an independent republic, the prompt closing with the Republic of a contract by which we acquired the necessary dominion and the necessary control of a strip fifty miles long by ten miles wide, through which we are now building the canal with an organization of machinery and men under competent engineers, insuring its completion within the next six years. Against Democratic opposition, and in the face of insurrection, inspired by their attitude, we have produced tranquillity in the Philippines, established a good government and are engaged in the greatest altruistic work that any nation ever undertook in uplifting eight millions of an Oriental people to a level of intelligence and self-restraint, enabling them to govern themselves. Cuba, that we once put on her feet, became involved in a revolution which by our intervention we succeeded in composing through the temporary assumption of control under our treaty rights with that island, and before this administration closes, Cuba will be returned to the government of the people.

The Republican party has pursued the consistent policy of maintaining an adequate army and navy to secure proper national defense and to give adequate weight to our voice in the international councils for international peace. We seek no conquest of other nations. We wish to avoid war in every honorable way, but we are not content to put ourselves in a position where we may be exposed to national humiliation and insult without the means of enforcing our honor and our rights.

We are a great nation. The world has not reached a millennium. Other nations are armed and have great naval and land forces at their command. If we would maintain national prestige, if we would have the influence to which a nation of our standing, population and wealth is entitled, we must maintain a reasonably large navy and we must have an army so organized as to form an efficient skeleton of a much larger army to be called into requisition in times of danger.

We have now an army of about 65,000 men. This is a very small army as compared with our population. It is smaller than the army was in the time of Washington or of Jefferson. The charge that the Army has been increased for the purpose of use in the suppression of domestic riots is utterly unfounded. The large camps are being established away from large cities where we can get an expanse of territory in order to permit of the modern drill and modern manœuvres.

Our coast defenses have not yet been completed. Our Army is not sufficiently large to permit the equipment of more than two-thirds of the batteries now ready for use upon our coasts. Clearly, if we have guns, we must have men to mount them.

The Navy is being gradually increased and the bluejackets and marines necessary for its equipment are being added to its enlisted force. The whole nation is in favour of an adequate military establishment. The Republican party is willing to pay the price. The Democratic party, as we shall see hereafter, is in favor of an adequate navy, but is opposed to paying for it.

Through the prestige obtained by the Spanish War, by the extension of our influence throughout the East and by our general foreign policy, we acquired influence sufficient to permit our President, Theodore Roosevelt, to act as the peacemaker of the world and bring the Russian-Japanese War to an end. In Santo Domingo, in Central America and South America, we have successfully bent our energies to bring into closer union, in interest and in sympathy with the United States, the Latin-American countries to the south of us. In China we have established the open door policy, by which we enjoy equal opportunities with other countries in dealing with that great empire.

By the system of irrigation of arid lands, we are reclaiming valuable portions of our Western government estate for the use of farmers. Through the Agricultural Department and through the Post-office Department we have greatly improved the condition of the farming community, enabling them by the scientific investigations of the Agricultural Department to economize the methods and to increase the product and the profits of the farm. Through the Post-office Department we have extended to the farmers of the community the rural free delivery, which brings them close into touch with urban communities, and which, with the suburban electric road and the telephone, have much ameliorated the hard conditions of farm life. We have increased the efficiency of the Army. We have added to the strength of the Navy. Steps are being taken under the active energy of the present Administration to a conservation of those natural resources, the forests, the water and the mining wealth of the country, so that they shall not be wantonly exhausted, but shall be preserved for the rational use of generations to come.

We as a party in State and nation have enacted more legislation for the special benefit and the relief of labor during the past two decades than any party in the history of the country. In President Harrison's day we adopted the safety appliance requirements for interstate railroads to reduce if possible the shocking loss of life and limb to the employees of those great arteries of commerce. We adopted the eight-hour law for Government workingmen, with the effect of giving an impetus to the reduction of hours of labor in all branches of industry, and in the present administration of Mr. Roosevelt we have added to the safety appliances required upon the railroads, we have shortened the hours during which railroad employees can be kept at work, and we have passed an employers' liability act for interstate railroads which abolished the defense of fellow-servant and the forfeiture of all rights of the employee to recover because of slight contributory negligence. We have adopted a model child labor bill for the District of Columbia, with a view of arousing the States to similar action. We have appropriated large sums of money to make the investigations into the cause of mining disasters. We have adopted the arbitration plan for settling the disputes between interstate railroads and their employees, and we have finally adopted a law recognizing the liability of the Government to make compensation for the injuries sustained by its employees in its service.

In the course of the prosperity of the last twelve years when expansion was going on so rapidly and a great many people were made rich quickly, it was natural that abuses should creep in, and they did creep in. Corporations with enormous wealth desired political influence to further their ends, and did not hesitate to use every means to command it. Trustees in the management of great financial funds proved in some instances to have been recreant to the trust. Revelations came, showing that the railroads of the country had fallen into a state of habitual lawlessness with respect to the granting of undue discriminations and rebates, and these rebates and undue discriminations were granted to the monopolizing trusts, and were the chief means of enabling them to destroy and cripple competition.

In this condition of affairs the Republican party through Theodore Roosevelt stepped into the breach to give expression to the moral awakening that such revelations had caused among the people. Legislation was introduced in the form of the Rate Bill, which, taken with the previous bill called the Elkins Bill, brought the railroads much more completely under the supervision and power of the Interstate Commerce Commission. Prosecutions under the Antitrust Law, which by the way, had been passed by a previous Republican administration, were begun with so much vigor that in one year there were more prosecutions under Theodore Roosevelt than in all the time since the act was passed in 1890. Not only was there a moral awakening among the people, but the legislation I referred to, the executive action, all had the effect to put fear in the hearts of the violators of the law and to bring about a condition with respect to the railroads in which to-day rebates and unlawful discriminations are practically abolished and a condition in which those combinations and corporations charged with being unlawful monopolies and obnoxious trusts are consulting the law with a view to keeping within its provisions.

The abolition of rebates and the prosecution of the trusts have so restrained their violation of law that competition is springing up where there was no competition before, and the great combinations of capital are keeping within their proper function, that of manufacturing, of carrying on the industries of the country, of distributing a very large wage fund, and of avoiding the use of those cunning devices which, taken with large aggregation of capital, have heretofore been used in the suppression of competition.

This condition has been brought about largely by the stand of Theodore Roosevelt and the action of the Republican Congress under his recommendation. The first Congress of his Administration passed more laws of a remedial and beneficial character than any Congress since the War. The Meat Inspection Bill, the Pure Food Bill, the Rate Bill, in addition to the labor legislation already referred to, make up a roll of efficient legislation that may well make proud the party responsible for it.

It is true that in the first session of the present Congress so much remedial legislation was not passed, and this has been made the basis for an assumption that in the next Congress there will be similar deliberation and hesitation. It must be remembered that legislation of this character does not pass all at once, but should have careful and minute consideration. The Rate Bill and the other measures which passed in the first Congress of the present administration were introduced in a previous Congress and had there failed. We must know that Congressmen are now going back to their constituents to receive a new mandate. We must know that they are going back to a constituency imbued with enthusiasm for the Roosevelt policies and filled with the determination that they shall prevail. Hence, we may take the declaration of the Republican platform in Chicago that the party approves the Roosevelt policies and insists upon their support in good faith by the representatives in Congress and the Executive, as an evidence that in the party itself there is that stern loyalty to the principles laid down by Theodore Roosevelt that will insure within the next Administration, if it is Republican, further steps onward toward the goal which he has set up for the American people.

The question of what additional legislation shall be adopted is, of course, a difficult one. We are certain that one of the evils from which this country has suffered in the past and which must be restricted is in the power of the managers of railroads to issue bonds and stocks under State corporations without proper supervision and without regard to the actual value of the property upon which they are secured. Therefore we are all agreed, and the Republican party so declared in convention assembled, that there must be Federal legislation placing under the control of some tribunal—probably the Interstate Commerce Tribunal—the issue of stocks and bonds by interstate railways to such an amount as is justified by the value of the property upon which the securities are to be issued.

Then there is a proposition to amend the Antitrust Law so as to make it more effective. The amendment which has struck the President with favor is an amendment by which all corporations which register and submit their books and business to the close supervision of the Department of Commerce and Labor shall be immune from prosecution for reasonable restraint of interstate trade. This, it is thought, will induce all corporations likely to violate the Antitrust Law to register.

The Democratic platform suggests the remedy that all companies manufacturing more than 25 percent of any product shall be required to take out a Federal license and thus be brought within the supervision of the Federal Government. I think this method is impracticable. It would be difficult to tell what such a statute meant, whether it would refer to a class of products or to particular articles, and it would make subject to license a great many small corporations that manufacture special articles, or patented articles that are not within the class of trusts and do not need supervision, because their output is so small and the business they do is negligible in the general business of the country. It is of the highest importance that we should limit the supervision and the necessity for examination to the corporations that have a temptation to violate the Antitrust Law. To impose the burden of a license or of close Federal supervision upon all the corporations that do interstate commerce business would be a burden so great as to disgust the public with the law. My own impression is that an examination into the statistics of the large manufacturing corporations, together with all their subsidiary corporations, will show it possible to fix a classification by the amount of capital invested in the business. For instance, that all corporations and combinations of corporations having a capital of more than a certain amount and doing an interstate commerce business should be required to submit reports of the business done by them, and to subject their books to frequent examination by government agents.

The machinery of the Government for the purpose of supervising such enterprises is inadequate. The bureaus in the Department of Commerce and Labor and in that of Justice should be enlarged. The jurisdiction of the Interstate Commerce Commission should be reduced so far as the railroads are concerned, so that the Commission shall exercise no administrative and prosecuting functions, but shall only act as the quasi-judicial tribunal upon the complaints made either by private individuals or by the Department of Commerce and Labor. Their jurisdiction might be further enlarged as a quasi-judicial tribunal to make orders for, and direct prosecutions of interstate corporations coming within the classification above named for violations of the Antitrust Law. Of course, if decisions of administrative tribunals are not acquiesced in, the courts are the final resort; but my own judgment from observation is that in most controversies, where there is a full understanding of the determination of the Government to be rigid, earnest and active in its policy of enforcing the law, it is quite possible to settle nearly all disputes by acquiescence of both parties in the judgment of administrative tribunals.

The Democratic platform recommends that all corporations manufacturing more than 50 percent of any product shall be required to cut down its plant, so that the product shall not exceed 50 percent of the total product of the country. This provision, easy to state, is most difficult to execute, for the same reason as the 25 percent limitation, because no one would know whether the limitation applied to one article or a class of articles. Men engaged in the business could not tell whether they were manufacturing more or less than 50 percent of the product, because it is necessarily dependent on the question of what others are manufacturing. Plants cannot be cut down as trees are by measuring 50 percent of the trunk from the ground to the top; and the whole proposition savors of that academic, impracticable character which is evidence that the proposition was inserted in the platform not for actual economic operation but merely to satisfy the demand for some specific remedy in an argument on the stump.

No one can deny who is at all familiar with the happenings of the last four years that this Administration has grappled the question of monopolies and railroad abuses as it has never been grappled before, and that this has been done with the assistance of a Republican Congress. Now that it has been done Mr. Bryan and the Democratic party step forward to say that it is in accordance with their previous recommendations, and that they and not Mr. Roosevelt and the Republican party are entitled to the credit for it. This is a characteristic difference between the parties. One party does the thing, the other party claims it because it talked about it.

Another thing the Republican party pledges itself to do, fixes the date when it will do, and tells you how it will do, is the revision of the tariff. The Dingley Tariff has served the country well, but its rates have become generally excessive. They have become excessive because conditions have changed since its passage in 1896. Some of the rates are probably too low, due also to a change of conditions. But on the whole, the tariff ought to be lowered, in accordance with the Republican principles and the policy that it has always upheld of protection of our industries. That is, every schedule ought to be arranged so that the tariff on the products of the factory, farm and mine shall be equal to the difference between the cost of their production in this country and the cost of their production abroad. This cost of production is made up by the cost of materials, the cost of labor and the manufacturer's interest and profit. It is not an easy thing, of course, to reach this difference. The examination to be made should be fair and impartial between the manufacturer and the consumer.

Now, Mr. Bryan is greatly concerned, and says that no such tariff revision can be made in view of the fact that the protected industries control the Republican party. I deny this. If there are protected industries that are enjoying too great profits under the present tariff, they would have opposed revision altogether. The movement in favor of revision has arisen within the Republican party, and is pressed forward by members of the Republican party. The revision which they desire is a revision which shall reduce excessive rates and at the same time preserve the industries of the country. It took some time, as it always does in a party, to crystallize this sentiment. It has been crystallized, and the party is determined to see that this revision shall go on by fixing the date when it is to begin and prescribing the rule by which it is to be carried on. I wish there to be no doubt in respect to the revision of the tariff. I am a tariff revisionist and have been one since the question has been mooted. The members of Congress who are elected this time are to be elected by constituencies that, we may infer from the action of the Republican Convention, are strongly in favor of a re-examination and a revision of the tariff.

Under those circumstances, we have the right to say that the revision will be made upon just and fair lines, and that the plighted faith of the party will be carried out as formulated in the platform. I do not mean to say that manufacturing interests will not, of course, try to use their influence with respect to the tariff. They can and ought to. From them we must get evidence as to what the cost of production is. But evidence must be taken from other sources, so that we shall have a fair and impartial hearing.

I am convinced that the whole Republican party is in earnest about this, and I do not hesitate to say that, as President of the United States, if I be elected, I shall use all the influence which I can legitimately use to bring about a full and perfect performance of the pledge.

Mr. Bryan and the Democratic platform propose a revision on tariff revenue lines. Mr. Bryan says, and the platform says, this shall be gradual. They thus prescribe no definite rule and leave it wholly to their discretion after the election, should they be chosen. Mr. Bryan cannot deny that substituting a revenue tariff for a protective tariff—a tariff for revenue, whether the change be gradual or not—necessarily wipes out some industries, and the course proposed therefore is, as Governor Hughes correctly said, a series of tariff tinkerings, step by step, lopping off the branches of industry one by one, keeping the country in a continued state of agitation, and paralyzing all enterprise and business. It is idle to suppose that in fixing a tariff for revenue there will not be some anxious interest by those whose business will be affected by the change, to prevent injury to one industry and to secure benefit to another.

Mr. Bryan attacks the Republican party for its extravagance and quotes from the Democratic platform to sustain his view. In the first place, taking the whole expenditure of the Government, and comparing it with the amount of wealth per capita, the percentage of cost of the Federal Government is less to-day than it ever was. In this respect, the Federal Government expenditures differ from the expenditures of counties, towns and cities, for as to them, the percentage of cost per wealth per capita has increased from year to year and from decade to decade. The answer to the complaint of a billion-dollar total of appropriations is that this is a billion-dollar country. The Federal Government has been called upon to enlarge its usefulness by spending money for many things which in times past were either not done at all or were left to the initiative of the States. We are spending $10,000,000 in the Agricultural Department alone to aid the farmer in knowledge of better agriculture. We are spending $37,000,000 for rural free delivery to make his lot more comfortable. We are enlarging the health departments of the United States. We are increasing the activities of the Government by the Pure Food Law, by the Meat Inspection Law, by the Rate Bill, by the prosecutions under the Antitrust Law. We are increasing the expenditures for waterways and intend to do still more in this way. We are increasing our Navy and are perfecting and equipping our coast defenses with men and guns. Now, we find the Democracy and Mr. Bryan occupying a characteristic attitude toward these expenditures. In order to please the Pacific Coast, he departed from the position he took in other campaigns in denouncing an imperialistic navy, and in order to get votes on the Pacific Coast he permitted a plank in favor of an "adequate" navy; but now he objects to the naval expenditures. In other words, he wants a navy enough to angle for votes with a plank in its favor, but he objects to paying for it.

But let us examine the specifications as to extravagance. The Democratic platform denounces the Administration for increasing the offices by 23,000 at a cost of $20,000,000 last year. As a matter of fact, the net increase in the offices was less than half, or 10,682, and the cost was $9,087,987. And what did the increase chiefly consist of? It was of about 7,000 enlisted men in the Navy to man our new ships and 3,000 in the Post-office Department to permit the expansion of that Department to meet the wants of the country in rural free delivery and other service. But the Democratic platform goes further. It says that in six years we have increased the civil service by 99,319 offices at a cost of $70,000,000. Let us see what the facts are. The net increase of offices in that time, instead of being what they say, was only 51,416, at a cost of $37,000,000. This increase was made up of 6,439 officers and men for coast defenses, 19,364 for the Navy, and about 20,000 in the Post-office Department. Certainly, we need our coast defenses properly equipped with men. As it is, we have not enough by 33 percent to equip our existing coast defense batteries with one shift of men. The increase in the Navy was not enough to man our ships, and a number had to go out of commission. The increase in the post-office service was necessary to meet the growth of business and was paid for by increased earnings.

This is all the Democratic attack amounts to. Their figures are too large by half, and when we examine the other half we find it to have been in directions to which even the Democrats do not object.

I have thus reviewed what the Republican party has done, and what in effect it promises to do. With respect to those policies known as Roosevelt policies, involving a closer supervision of the railways, a closer supervision of the large corporations engaged in interstate commerce, and a continuance of the prosecutions for violation of law, all I have to say is that, as President of the United States, it will not only be my purpose, but it will be my pride, to clinch the Roosevelt policies by energetic executive action, and by the earnest recommendation to Congress of such constructive measures as may make the supervision of these great business interests of the country effective to prevent abuses; to furnish guidance for honest and legitimate business managers, and to disturb legitimate business as little as possible. If ever the party earned the verdict of "well done" by the record of the last seven years, and the reward of a renewed mandate of power, it is the Republican party under Theodore Roosevelt, and I do not hesitate to ask for that mandate under my leadership because my association with Mr. Roosevelt, my participation in much of his Administration as his adviser, and as his agent, have enabled me to know what the task is, enabled me to understand the principles that have governed him in his course, and given me something of the enthusiasm and joy of accomplishment that has made him such a matchless leader in these reforms.

Turning now to the other picture, what is it that we have to expect from Mr. Bryan? Have we anything to expect but what he promises? Have we anything to expect but what is based upon his eloquence and his adroitness as a public critic? Has he ever given any practical demonstration of his ability to meet problems and solve them? Has he ever done anything but formulate propositions in his closet of an utterly impracticable character, largely with a view of attracting votes by their plausibility, and very little with a view of their actual operation? "By their fruits ye shall know them." What is the history of Mr. Bryan? It is from beginning to end a record of failures on public questions. We find him first in Congress, in the second administration of Mr. Cleveland, a member of the Ways and Means Committee, and most active in formulating the provisions of the Gorman-Wilson Tariff Bill. After five months' debate, it passed both Houses and came to Mr. Cleveland in such a shape that he denounced it as a piece of perfidy. It levelled the industries of this country to the ground. It threw out of employment millions of wage-earners. It destroyed all business profit. Farm products for lack of a market fell to a point never so low in forty years. Coxey's army marched from the West to Washington to protest against a government under which such things were possible.

And then, after having assisted in this suicidal policy, after the country was nearly dead, after the farmers and wage-earners were staggering under debt and mortgage, penury and almost starvation, Mr. Bryan defeats the efforts of the only really great Democrat that they have had in the party for many years, Grover Cleveland, and hurls at him billings-gate denunciation, for what reason? Because he opposes Mr. Bryan's pet hobby, that of the free coinage of silver, without the consent of any other nation. Mr. Bryan announced that the gold standard had slain its tens of thousands, where protection had slain its thousands, and so he abandoned the issue of protection and free trade, of tariff for revenue, which now so attracts him, and he went into the business of trying to persuade the people of this country to resort to the dishonest method of paying off their debts by issuing a debased money which would be equivalent to the payment of what the nation and the people owe at the rate of fifty cents on the dollar. Repudiation always has an attraction for those who are laboring under debt. Never in the history of the country was there a time when that pernicious proposition could have appealed to the people as it did in 1896. It was pressed home by all forms of specious argument, and the temptation was dangled under the noses of the good people of this country to wipe off their honest obligations, not by payment in the coin in which they were contracted, but by legislative act. Fortunately the honor and the good sense of the American people revolted. Fortunately the laboring man saw the payment of his debts with the fifty-cent dollar was only one side of the picture, and that when it meant that his hard-earned wages were to be paid in the same kind of coin, he was the creditor, and that the repudiation was against him and not in his favor.

In that campaign Mr. Bryan prophesied that the continuation of the gold standard meant uncertainty in employment of labor and hardship to the wage-earner; that it would send down the price of farm products—wheat below fifty cents, corn below twenty cents, and oats to five cents.

He did not have to live two years to see every prophecy that he made in that campaign refuted by the fact.

Then there came on the campaign of 1900. In that campaign he still adhered to his free-silver fallacy, and still went about the country trying to explain why it was that the continuation of the gold standard had not resulted in the disasters he had prophesied. But lest the issue of free silver had become a little shopworn, he brought out as a paramount issue that of anti-imperialism. He announced that if he were not elected in the next election, patriotism would have ceased to be in this country, the celebration of the Fourth of July would become but a memory, and that liberty would die. His agitation of this question continued the war in the Philippines against the authority of the United States for nearly two years longer, and many a poor fellow who lost his life in the service of his country in those far-distant islands owes it directly to the inspiration which the opposition of the Democracy under Mr. Bryan made to the policy of Mr. McKinley in the Philippines. He was beaten on these issues, and we continue to celebrate the Fourth of July with fervor.

At the end of the next four years Mr. Parker was nominated. Mr. Bryan still insisted on inserting in the platform a clause in favor of free silver, but it was left out. He then joined with Mr. Parker in making the paramount issue the tyranny of Theodore Roosevelt, executive usurpation and militarism. He denounced Mr. Roosevelt as completely subject to corporate interests, and held up to the country the dangers of war to which it would be subject under a Roosevelt administration. Although the same policy was being pursued in the Philippines as before, imperialism had ceased to be then a paramount issue.

The prophecy which Mr. Bryan made with reference to the warlike tendencies of Mr. Roosevelt and to his subjection to corporate influence, he had only to wait, as he had had to wait in previous instances when he made a prophecy, some two years to find them utterly refuted. For never in the history of the world has any chief executive had such a triumph in making peace as Theodore Roosevelt in the Russian-Japanese War, in Central America, in Santo Domingo and in Cuba; and never in the history of the country has there been such a complete triumph over corporate influences as that which the courage, the honesty and the persistence of Theodore Roosevelt have wrought during the present Administration.

In the campaign of 1904, and in previous campaigns, Mr. Bryan had denounced militarism and imperialism, but this year he was advised that the visit of our Navy to the Pacific Coast had aroused such an interest in the Navy, had made it so popular on that coast that his Pacific friends persuaded him to approve a plank in the platform for an adequate navy for the protection of the Pacific Coast. Just what he means by this it is a little difficult to tell. What the Republican party means by it is clear. It means an increase in the present forces of the Navy, and yet with characteristic inconsistency Mr. Bryan, as already said, attacks the Republican party for making suitable appropriations for the increase of our naval force.

In 1906 Mr. Bryan went around the world, and his return was heralded with the statement that in his visit around the world he had so gained information and knowledge that he had become safe and sane, that he was a conservative, and all the Democratic party awaited his coming with great interest. Immediately upon his arrival he dispelled this erroneous impression by declaring that he was convinced that the only solution of the railroad problem ultimately would be government ownership. He has previously declared in favor of a national initiative and referendum and also in favor of the election of Federal judges. All these most radical propositions have now been excluded from the Democratic platform. They do not meet such popular approval as to justify their being brought forward as a means of acquiring office in this campaign, but they illustrate the character of the man who proposes them, they show the instability and variability of his views, and they justify the fear that so many people of this country have in respect to the danger to which the public weal may be exposed should he be put at the helm as the pilot.

And now, with this record of promises and prophecies unfulfilled for a period of twelve years, with this record of a hunt for an issue upon which to achieve the Presidency, with this record of repudiation, of negation and of running away from national responsibilities, Mr. Bryan comes forward and asks that the people now give him an opportunity to put into operation new reforms in respect to trusts and in respect to guaranty of bank deposits, wholly untried, wholly theoretical, and on their face bearing evidence of their impracticability and of having been devised by the ready brain of one looking for plausible arguments rather than real reforms. He only in a qualified way approves the postal savings banks recommended by the

Republican platform, which is a tried and proved means of encouraging the wage-earner and small farmer to make deposits in a bank absolutely secure; but much prefers a system which takes a man's money to pay another man's default and which, instead of strengthening our banking system, will break it down by destroying the value of banking character and experience and capital, and offering inducement to reckless and speculative bankers without character or capital.

Last fall we had a panic. I think that there is a consensus of conservative opinion as to the cause of it. It is that we had expended in every business direction and had increased the amount of capital in fixed investments to such a point as to almost exhaust the sources of supply of further capital. The profits from the investments were not sufficient to make new capital as rapidly as it was required, and it became impossible to borrow money even on the best security for new enterprises. In addition to this, the revelations of the bad management of certain of our corporations, of the lawless conduct of others, and of the lack of proper supervision and control of many financial enterprises, together with the feeling properly aroused against great corporations that had abused their privileges and sought to obtain undue advantage through political control, frightened those who had capital to invest. There came a stringency, a panic, and a subsequent depression. The panic differed from previous panics in that the farmers continue to be prosperous; their products are selling at a very high price, and nothing is wanting but a restoration of confidence and the investment of capital to bring about the old prosperous conditions.

The record of Mr. Bryan and his character, as it is understood by a twelve years' acquaintance with him, have impressed the business community of this country and those whose judgments determine whether or not capital shall be invested that he is not a safe man with whom to try experiments in government; that he loves financial theories that are full of sophistry and are impractical; that he advances propositions with but little sense of responsibility as to how they may be carried out in practice, and that he gives but little attention to the welfare of the conservative business community in his suggestions of reform. Certainly his record justifies this judgment of him by the business men. If he were to be elected, unquestionably because of his record, however much now he may seek to pose as a conservative—because of his record, because of the failure of the theories which he has proposed for the last twelve years, his election will mean a paralysis in business, a halt and hesitation until it is known what he is going to do with the power to be entrusted to him, and a consequent permanent continuance of the depression with which the country has been afflicted for now nearly a year. The present gradual advance toward prosperity would cease, and we should have a recurrence of the disastrous business condition of the last Democratic administration.

8

The Railroads and the Courts

Delivered at Orchestra Hall, Chicago, Illinois, September 23, 1908

My Fellow-citizens:

I am glad to meet so many members of organized railroad labor. I think it is generally conceded that railroad orders, or "brotherhoods" as they are called, have been conducted with marked ability and with the greatest usefulness, not only to their members but to the community at large, including their employers, the railroads; and I have accepted this opportunity to address an audience of members of the brotherhoods in order that I may take up a question which has been given great prominence in this campaign, and in which I must say that every effort has been made unjustly to arouse the prejudice of organized labor against the Republican party and its candidate.

In the first place, I wish to affirm, without fear of contradiction, that the Republican party has done vastly more than the Democratic party, both in State and National legislation, for the protection and in the interest of labor. It passed in General Harrison's administration the eight hour law for government workmen and gave an impetus to a reduction of hours in other employments. The Safety Appliance Act, by which railroads engaged in interstate commerce were required to make provision for the safety of their employees, and thus to reduce the shocking loss of life and limb among railroad employees, was passed in the same Administration. Amendments to this act making more detailed specifications for improvements in safety appliances, including especially the fire pan, have been passed in the present Administration. An act for the promotion of arbitration between the railways and their employees in interstate commerce is also one of those acts of beneficence to both employer and employee. Under the common law, as declared by the Supreme Court of the United States, if an employee was injured in the service of a railway company, and the injury arose from the negligence of a fellow-servant, he could not recover damages. Again, if he was guilty of the slightest negligence contributing to the accident, his suit failed. The last Congress enacted a law which was declared unconstitutional, and then in its second session reenacted the law to avoid the constitutional objections. By this act a railway employee who brings suit for damages against the company cannot now be defeated on the ground that the negligence was the negligence of a fellow-servant. If he is shown to be guilty of negligence himself in a slight degree, he does not forfeit his right of action, but it is left to the jury to apportion the damages and reduce them as equity shall justify.

In addition to this, a law limiting the hours of labor of interstate railway employees has been passed, as well as a model child labor law in the District of Columbia; and money has been appropriated for the purpose of making investigation into the cause of the dreadful mining injuries. Heretofore all persons working for the Government have been denied any right to compensation for injuries received in the Government employ, no matter through whose negligence. A bill was passed by the last session of Congress providing for compensation to Government employees in such cases. It is an inadequate law and will doubtless be improved by coming Congresses, but the principle that the Government will not pay compensation for injuries received in its employ has now been abrogated, and we may look ultimately for exactly the same compensation in government cases as where the employer is an individual or a corporation.

The record of the Republican party, therefore, I think may be looked to with confidence as a conclusive proof that that party has always been friendly to labor, and has never failed in its duty when called upon to enact suitable and protective laws.

An issue, however, has arisen as to the attitude of the two parties on the subject of injunctions in labor disputes.

I propose now to take up first my personal relation to this question. It fell to my lot to be a Judge of the Superior Court of Cincinnati for three years and a Judge of the United States Circuit Court for the Sixth District, including Michigan, Ohio, Kentucky and Tennessee, for eight years, and during that time I had to consider a number of important cases involving the rights of labor and the rights of the employer, as well as the practice in equity with reference to the issuing of injunctions in such cases. The first case was not an injunction suit at all. A boss bricklayer quarreled with the union, and their members who were in his employ struck. In order to embarrass him the union notified all the local dealers in materials that they would boycott any firm which furnished him with material. Moores & Co. had a contract to deliver to this boss bricklayer a lot of lime. In order to avoid trouble they secured from him a release from the contract; but he sent his wagon to the freight station and bought lime out of the car where Moores & Co. sold lime to any one who applied. The walking delegate of the union discovered it, and a boycott was begun.

Moores & Co. were prevented from selling to their usual customers any lime or other material for a great number of months, and suffered a severe financial loss to their business. They sued for damages and the case was tried before a jury. The jury returned a verdict for $2,500. Now, gentlemen, in that case I held and decided with two colleagues that a secondary boycott was an unlawful injury, and that whether it was perpetrated by laboring men or otherwise. That is the law today and, my friends, it ought to be the law. I understand that the railway orders, generally, acquiesce in the proposition that it is not wise to use such a secondary boycott as an instrument in industrial disputes. I know that this is not the view of Mr. Gompers, but I am glad to know that there is a difference in organized labor upon this question. Certainly no more cruel instrument of tyranny was ever adopted than this secondary boycott.

Now, what was the second case in 1903? In that case the Toledo & Ann Arbor Railroad was in a dispute with its employees, who were members of the Brotherhood of Locomotive Engineers, and a strike by the engineers followed. It was understood by the Toledo & Ann Arbor road that the brotherhood engineers on the Lake Shore road were going to refuse to haul their cars, and that the Lake Shore road for that reason would acquiesce in this action. Accordingly the Toledo & Ann Arbor road applied to Judge Ricks to enjoin the Lake Shore Railroad Company, its officers and employees, from refusing to haul Toledo & Ann Arbor cars. He did so in accordance with the interstate commerce law, which requires one railroad engaged in interstate commerce to haul the cars of another railroad delivered to it, and imposes this duty not only on the railroad itself but upon the officers and employees. There was no order issued which required engineers to stay in the employ of the Lake Shore road. The order only required them, so long as they remained on their engines and in the employ of the Lake Shore road, to comply with the law and haul Toledo & Ann Arbor cars. After this, Mr. Arthur, the head of the Brotherhood of Locomotive Engineers, complying with a secret rule, No. 12, then in force in the order, which forbade the engineers on one road, members of the order, to haul the cars of another road when the order had a strike on the latter road, issued a notice to the engineers of the Lake Shore that the strike on the Toledo & Ann Arbor was approved as required by the rules of the order, and that they should proceed to enforce rule No. 12, which meant that they should refuse to haul the cars of the Toledo & Ann Arbor road. In other words, this order which he issued by telegram was a direct order to them to violate the Federal statute and to compel the Lake Shore road as a third person not interested in the controversy between the Toledo & Ann Arbor road and its former employees to assist their employees in their fight with that road. It was a secondary boycott, and it was a direct violation of the Federal statute which imposed a punishment by fine and imprisonment for its violation. I required Mr. Arthur to withdraw the telegram which he had issued to his men in respect to rule No. 12, and within a very short period I gave him a hearing. Mr. Arthur had promptly complied with my order and never did disobey it. My own impression always was that Mr. Arthur was glad to have it decided that such a rule as rule 12 was illegal. At all events, the Brotherhood of Locomotive Engineers then repealed the rule and it has never been enforced so far as I know.

I submit that the Brotherhood of Locomotive Engineers, in repealing rule No. 12 and condemning the use of the secondary boycott in such cases, justifies and vindicates fully the conclusion that I reached in that case, on the action that I took. The repeal of rule 12 brought the Brotherhood completely within the law and instead of being lawbreakers they became its conservators.

The third case was the Phelan case. It grew out of the attempt of the American Railway Union and Eugene Debs to starve the country by stopping all the railroads and thus compel the Pullman Company to pay higher wages to its employees. Neither the starving country nor the railroads had control over Mr. Pullman. They had no power to control him in any way or to compel him to change the terms upon which he employed his labor. Some railroads had contracts with him for carrying his cars. They were not justified in breaking those contracts. In other words, the action against the railroad companies by Debs and his lieutenant, Phelan, was a secondary boycott. At this time the Cincinnati Southern Railroad, 336 miles from Cincinnati to Chattanooga, was being operated by a receiver under my orders as United States Circuit Judge. Phelan knew this and was warned of it. He held meetings of the Cincinnati Southern Railroad employees, and advised them to strike and tie up the road, and by hints and winks and side remarks, he instigated them to violence, and to attack the men who stayed upon the engines and who worked the trains, and who refused to obey his call to leave the railway. You may remember that in that strike the regular Brotherhood did not join, because they did not believe in a sympathetic and aimless strike of that character. Nevertheless the strikers, acting under the instigation of Phelan, broke the heads of members of the Brotherhood locomotive engineers and firemen who stuck to their engines and attempted to carry on the business of the railroad. The chief residence of the employees was Ludlow, Kentucky, and it became entirely unsafe for the Brotherhood engineers and firemen of the receivers to go from the railway to their houses in Ludlow. On an affidavit charging him with contempt in attempting by such methods to defeat the order of court directing the receiver to run the road, he was brought into court. At the same time he was enjoined from continuing his obstruction and the time for hearing of the contempt proceedings was set in accordance with his desire. He employed counsel and for ten or twelve days I tried the case. Meantime, during the trial he continued his course. The evidence clearly established his guilt. His defiance of the court's order during the trial was flagrant and deliberate and tended to destroy the court's authority. I, therefore, sentenced him to jail for six months. It was necessary that this man who was inflicting loss not only upon the stockholders of the road but also upon the public, who was subjecting to lawless violence the Brotherhood engineers and firemen of the road, and who was holding the administration of justice up to contempt, should be punished in an orderly way.

I can understand how a man like Debs, a socialist tending to anarchy, who believes that modern society is established on a thoroughly wrong basis, that property ought to be divided equally, that everything ought to be run by the Government, should be in favor of such a disturbance as that which he created by bringing about the strikes and tying up the railroads as he did; but I cannot understand how intelligent and law-abiding members of the railroad orders entertaining the views which I am told they do entertain with reference to the boycott and with reference to violations of law in industrial disputes, can object to the course which was taken by me in these cases in employing all the lawful authority I had to prevent the injuries which were threatened and to bring about a lawful state of affairs.

There was one more injunction suit to which I made reference but in which the operation of the injunction was not against laboring people but against a combination of iron pipe manufacturers who, residing in some eleven States, divided up the territory, and by their agreements maintained the prices of iron pipe at an exorbitant figure, monopolized the whole production within those States, and divided the profits of this arrangement between the members of the combination. A suit was brought in the Circuit Court, and an application made by the United States for an injunction to enjoin the combination from proceeding and to break it up. The Circuit Judge held that there was no power to issue such an injunction and no jurisdiction in the court to grant such a remedy. I sat in the Court of Appeals to entertain an appeal by the Government from the decision of the Circuit Court and rendered the opinion of the Circuit Court of Appeals. We there decided that an injunction would issue; the injunction did issue and the combination was broken up. The case was subsequently carried to the Supreme Court of the United States, and the judgment was affirmed. I merely instance this to show that the injunction works both ways, and that it is useful both in keeping lawless laboring men and lawless capitalists within the law.

The principles laid down in this case, known as the Addyston Pipe case, are the principles upon which the Antitrust Law is now being enforced under the present Administration.

The law laid down in each of the labor cases I have referred to is in accordance with the policy now pursued by the railroad orders. Mr. Bryan says I am the father of injunctions in industrial causes. This is not true. The use of the injunction was in accordance with precedent in a number of cases which I cited, both in the Arthur case and in the Phelan case. I am not apologizing for what I did in these cases, for they were in accordance with my duty as a judge. I have merely gone into them to explain to you what they were in order to ask you whether they make a basis for the claim that I am hostile to labor organizations and opposed to the laboring men.

In these cases, I attempted to state with as great fulness as possible the rights and wrongs of employer and employee in these labor disputes; that men had the right to strike; that they had the right and duty to unite in order that they might present a solid front against their employer and deal with him on a level and not be subject to the disadvantage to which one laborer would be put in dealing with a powerful employer; that they had the right to select their officers and accept their advice with reference to what they should do; that they had the right to accumulate funds in order to support those of their number who had withdrawn from the employ of the employer; that they could withdraw from the association with their employer and have all their colleagues do the same thing, but they might not injure the property of their employer, and they might not injure his business by the secondary boycott.

Another point which I distinctly decided in these cases was that no temporary restraining order or injunction could issue to prevent a man's leaving the employ of a railway, and therefore that no injunctions could issue to restrain men from acting in concert and going on a strike.

The statement of the law in these labor decisions was used and cited on behalf of labor organizations in the case before Judge Adams against the Gould roads, in which the Gould lines attempted to enjoin the Order of Railway Conductors and the other railway orders from agreeing to strike and following the orders of their officers. Judge Adams first issued the injunction, and then on the authority of the principles laid down by me in the Phelan and Arthur cases, he dissolved the injunction and the strike was won by the railway orders. I only instance this to show that the principles that I laid down were not antagonistic to labor, and they were used by labor to defend its rights in a subsequent controversy.

Objection is made to the use of the injunction in such disputes. All I have to say on that point is that precedent justifies it, and that the man whose business is injured by unlawful action of former employees frequently has no other remedy which is at all adequate. He is just as much entitled to that remedy against striking laborers as he would be against any other members of the community who inflict similar injury. The character of the injury inflicted upon his business, which consists in constant interference with his customers until the customers are frightened or driven away, is the basis for resorting to injunction. A suit for damages or a criminal prosecution for one of such acts would be utterly lacking in efficacy. The owner of the business, whether railroad business or any other, is entitled to be protected in his pursuit of it and to immunity from unlawful injury to it. To take away from him the remedy by injunction which has always been his, merely because it sometimes leads to the punishment of those who violate the injunction without a trial by jury, is to introduce into the law class legislation in favor of employees and laboring men, and it is to take them out of the ordinary operation of civil remedies because they are laborers. I say that that kind of class legislation is pernicious; that laborers themselves ought not to wish it; that it weakens the powers of the court which are just as necessary to the preservation of the rights of laborers as of other persons, and that it is a short-sighted policy. The weakening of the power of the courts will not be taken advantage of so much by the laboring men as by the rich violator of the law, because he can employ cunning and astute counsel to enable him to take advantage of every such weakness.

Objection is made to the issuing of injunctions without notice. There is opportunity for abuse in such a practice, though there are cases when no other remedy seems adequate. I have been willing, nevertheless, to adopt a rule by which notice shall be required before the issuing of any injunction, temporary or otherwise. The Republican Convention, however, thought it wiser that the best present practice should be embodied in a statute in order to bring the matter to the attention of the court, and that in that way future abuses could be avoided. I hope and believe that this is true.

Under the Republican platform a statute can pass and ought to pass which shall not allow a temporary restraining order to issue and have effect for more than forty-eight hours unless a hearing can be had during that forty-eight hours extending the operation of the injunction.

The Democratic platform does not give any remedy with respect to notice. It merely resolves that injunctions ought not to issue in industrial disputes where they would not issue in other disputes. This is either meaningless or deceitful. If by it is meant that they ought not to issue in industrial disputes at all, then it recommends class legislation. If it means that they ought only to issue in industrial disputes on the same principle and under the same circumstances governing their issue in other disputes, then every one concurs. No one ever contended otherwise.

The provision in the Democratic platform, that a trial by jury shall be allowed in all cases in which a charge of contempt is made for violation of the orders of court outside of the presence of the judge, would greatly weaken the power of the court. A witness subpœnaed could not be punished for failure to respond to the subpœna until a jury was summoned to find that he had received the subpœna and had disobeyed it. A juror summoned and failing to respond could not be punished for failing to respond until a jury met to determine whether he had received the summons and whether he had not responded. A final judgment requiring the defendant to do something or not to do something, if the defendant declined to do either, could not be enforced without summoning a jury to determine all the facts of the case. In other words, after the case had been taken through all the courts to the Supreme Court, and the principles affirmed and then sent down for execution against a recalcitrant defendant, judgment could not be enforced except after the uncertainties of a trial by jury. Thus to introduce a jury trial between a final order and its enforcement and between the routine orders bringing witnesses and jurors into court would so hamper the administration of justice as to make the courts a laughing-stock. It may be popular to suggest such a change. It may attract the support and approval of those who do not understand its real effect; but so long as I have power of expression and without regard to how it may affect me politically, I shall lift my voice in protest against such a destructive step in our judicial procedure.

Mr. Bryan says that this proposed amendment by which a jury trial is to be introduced in contempt cases was approved by Senator Sherman of Ohio, Senator Allison of Iowa, Senator Hale of Maine, Senator Hawley of Connecticut, Senator Morrill of Vermont and Senator Nelson of Minnesota. I deny it, and I challenge Mr. Bryan to produce the proof of it. The fact is that the bill, as originally proposed, left the question of trial by jury in the discretion of the court. Senator Butler introduced the amendment by which it was made mandatory to have such a trial, and the bill and the amendment were opposed by Senator Platt of Connecticut, who was senior Republican member of the Judiciary Committee, and in whose opinion it is reasonable to infer that the Senators named by Mr. Bryan concurred, for he was of course Republican leader in judicial matters. The bill was passed by a *viva voce* vote without a roll call in a Democratic Senate, and there is nothing in the record to show the fact to be as Mr. Bryan states it.

I have been considering and discussing in your presence the decisions which I have rendered as a judge, in which I was bound by the law as I understood it and in which I was called upon to decide impartially on the facts presented to me. It has been sought to give the impression that this record of mine as a judge shows that I am unfriendly to labor. Nothing could be further from the fact. No one that I know has more sympathy with the laboring man, no one that I know is more anxious for legislation which will enable the wage-earner to maintain himself in the struggle for a livelihood and in his relations with a powerful employer. My relations to labor have not been confined to decisions upon the bench. As the executive in charge of the work on the Panama Canal I have had under me for four years upwards of thirty thousand laborers. It has given me pleasure to devote a great deal of time to the consideration of the welfare, as well as of the pay of the men employed under the Government in that great enterprise.

When I had charge of the matter, I spared no effort to see to it that the complaints of the men were thoroughly investigated, and, where they were well founded, that the ground of the complaint should be removed. I had there to consider the question of wages, had there to consider the questions of accommodations of laborers' quarters, and of all those details that in a labor colony necessarily come up for decision. And I have not the slightest hesitation in inviting the attention of the laboring men of the country to the recent report of a commission appointed by President Roosevelt as to the favorable conditions that have prevailed with respect to the employees of the Government on the Isthmus.

I have had occasion in the Philippines to deal with labor questions there, and I feel very confident that no one at all cognizant of the situation will charge that in my administration of the office of Governor of the Islands I was not fully alive to the interests of the laboring man, anxious to support the dignity of labor, and ready to extend the helping hand of the Government whenever it was possible to relieve the burden of the wage-earner, to stimulate his ambition to accomplish more, and to make him a respected and influential member of the community.

Should I be elected President, it will be one of my pleasantest duties to give attention to legislation needed in the interest of labor, as I have done during the present Administration as an advisor of the President.

The number of injunctions that have been issued in the case of railroad strikes can be counted on the fingers of one hand, and I venture to say that there are very few within the sound of my voice who have any practical knowledge of the operation of injunctions. The number issued against railroads and other corporations to restrain them from violations of law are much more numerous. The question which organized railroad labor men have to answer is whether, for what is today an academic reason, and one which really affects their relations to their employer in no substantial way at all, they propose to put in power a political party with a leader whose election will be regarded by all business men as a menace to their interests and a threat against returning prosperity. Now that this is a fact there is not the slightest doubt. You may ascertain it by inquiry, and the reason for the fact is not far to find. Mr. Bryan's public career began as a member of Congress in the sessions from '92 to '96. In the first session of his service was enacted the Gorman-Wilson Tariff Bill, and he was very prominent in urging its adoption and very jubilant over its passage. The result of the Gorman-Wilson Tariff Bill was to prostrate the industries of the country, and we had a four years' depression lasting up to 1897, the like of which has not been seen for years in this country. Wages went down, strikes followed, and an industrial depression that led to great suffering, especially on the part of the wage-earner. Mr. Bryan then came forward and announced that while protection had killed its thousands, the gold standard had killed its tens of thousands, and proposed that we should depart from the gold standard and adopt a silver dollar, which would enable us to pay all our debts in just half the amount in which they were contracted. The direct effect of this would have been to cut wages one-half, and in the general disaster and paralysis following there would have been a constant conflict on the part of labor with employers in order to restore wages to a proper equivalent under the gold standard. Mr. Bryan prophesied that if we continued on the gold standard and did not adopt the free coinage of silver, it would result in the greatest injury to labor. His prophesies were entirely refuted. There came on after the adoption of the gold standard, after the repeal of the Gorman-Wilson Bill, and the passage of the Dingley Bill, such a period of prosperity for twelve years as had never been seen in the world before. Wages and the standard of living of the laboring man were never so high. At the end of another four years Mr. Bryan came forward again proposing free coinage of silver in the face of the refutation, by the facts, which had been brought to his previous theories. Mr. Bryan proposed to substitute for the present protective policy, upon which the whole business of the country is based, a revenue tariff to be reached gradually by steps. I do not propose to stop to discuss the benefit of protection. For forty years the country has been on a protective system. Every well-sustained threat to depart from that system has brought financial disaster, and such a change is the main part of Mr. Bryan's platform in this campaign. In 1906, when Mr. Bryan came back from Europe and many of his party received him with the hope that he had acquired conservatism by his travels, he made the announcement that he was in favor of government ownership of railroads and was convinced that this must be the ultimate settlement of the railroad question. It was received by many of his party with disapproval, and so far for the time being he has postponed it as a political issue, but that he believes it is evidenced by what he said at the time, and no one can doubt that the whole tendency of his economic and political views is in that direction. I do not know how the railroad employees would like government ownership. I should think that they would view such a suggestion with great alarm. I am unalterably opposed to it. It would place too vast a power in the control of the President. It would lead to a management of railroads not nearly so effective as that which we have under private ownership, and it would involve the Government in an enormous debt. It would make railroad employees Government servants and would subject them to the dangers of political supervision in a way that certainly would be most inimical to their interests. It would revolutionize the whole vast railroad system of the country.

I submit that a gentleman whose record and whose propositions are thus shown to have been so actually inimical to the interests of labor and whose economic views are so utterly out of keeping with the sound and conservative principles of business, may well be considered by all business men and all workingmen, if he is elevated to the Presidency, a menace to the restoration of prosperity. We are all in the same boat, business men, workingmen, capitalists and professional men. We are all dependent upon the confidence which in the future will induce those who have capital to invest it, if we are to have a return to prosperity.

The whole country is dependent upon the prosperity of the railroads. The railroads need money to keep their lines in proper repair, to make necessary reconstruction and to continue the new construction to meet the demands of business. Unless they can borrow money for reconstruction there is not the demand for the manufacture of railway supplies that is necessary to keep business good in the country. The truth is that the railroads are the greatest single market that we have for manufactured products. We are all interested, therefore, that the credit of the railroads should be such as to enable them to borrow the money with which to carry on this constructive work.

We are interested that legislation against the railroads should be just and only properly restrictive. We are interested that there should not be unjust and drastic legislation preventing their earning proper income. We are all interested, of course, that they should charge only proper rates, but we are also interested that they should not be made to do business on less than just rates. I have noticed with a great deal of interest that the railroad laboring men are beginning to realize that the prosperity of the railroads is as much in their interest as it is in the interest of the stockholders and the officers of the road, and that they propose hereafter to be heard upon the political issue as to the character of the legislation that shall be passed with reference to the regulation of railroads. With this direct interest that railroad laboring men have in the prosperity of railroads, can they not see that it is of the utmost importance to prevent the election of the man whose record will make returning confidence and prosperity impossible?

We have passed through a financial panic and industrial depression. It differs from most panics which have occurred in the history of the country in that the farmers are in a most prosperous condition, and nothing seems lacking to the coming of good business within a few months after the panic but a restoration of confidence. Is it not apparent to you, therefore, that the election of Mr. Bryan to the powerful office of President, with his unstable financial theories and his uncertain economic propositions, will convince every one having capital to invest that the business future of the country is uncertain and that it is safer to withhold his money? Mr. Bryan says that this cry of the full dinner pail has been worked overtime. It was worked to great advantage in the previous campaigns, and properly so. The event justified the claim of the Republican party, for prosperity and a full dinner pail followed each election of a Republican President against the contention of Mr. Bryan. The present panic thus far has been a short one and there is not the slightest reason why, if the Republican party is continued in power, it will not lose its severity. I submit to those most interested, to this intelligent audience, that this is the issue of the full dinner pail that ought to make them for a third time reject Mr. Bryan's claim to be elected to the Presidency as a helpful friend of the workingman.

9

A Pledge of Tariff Reform

Delivered at Milwaukee, Wisconsin, September 24, 1908

I agree with Mr. Bryan that one important issue in this campaign is the revision of the tariff. Both parties concur in the view that it must be done, and the question is, "How shall it be done?" When it is settled how it shall be done, it is easy from the platforms of the parties to determine which party ought to do it. The Republican party since its birth has constantly been an advocate of the protective system. The Democratic party, not so consistently, but still on the whole, has been an advocate of a system of tariff for revenue only.

The principle of protection as upheld by the Republican party is that in raising the revenues of the Government from the customs it is proper to encourage and maintain diversified industries in this country instead of limiting the occupations and business to a few branches in which this country has the advantage over other countries and instead of being dependent on other countries for the purchase of goods which they can manufacture at less price than we do.

The measure of the protection to be offered by the tariff has usually been stated to be the difference between the cost of production abroad and in this country. The system of protection as developed here has resulted in a very high standard of wages, as compared with the wages of other countries, and a corresponding high standard of living among the laboring people. In this country too there is a different rate of interest on investments in active business to be treated in the manufacturing business as normal manufacturing profit. The manufacturer's profit necessarily differs in this country from what it is abroad. So, too, the raw materials which enter into the manufacture of the product differ in cost here and abroad. The measure of protection is the difference between the cost of production here and abroad, including the difference in the cost of material, the difference in the standard of wages, and the difference in the manufacturer's profit.

I cannot state what protection means more effectively than to quote from a speech by Congressman Hill of Connecticut, a member of the Ways and Means Committee of the House. He says:

"Protection assumes that it is better for this nation to add its labor and brains to its own raw materials and sell the finished product rather than to exhaust its natural resources to furnish employment to the labor and brains of other nations. It believes that a variety of industries utilizing all kinds of skill and all grades of labor is more beneficial to the nation as a whole than a few primitive pursuits which would draw the masses to a common level. It realizes that every step taken in the process of the development of a raw product, is a step forward in the progress of the nation, and this nation has learned in its own experience that economic self-reliance is its surest defense in war and its best asset in times of peace."

I do not intend to go into an argument as to the advantage of the protective system over the free trade or revenue tariff system, because it seems to me that the action of the country in the last forty-eight years has sufficiently demonstrated the correctness of our position as stated by Mr. Hill. The Democratic policy is to put a low tax on everything imported and encourage large purchases abroad, throwing open the home market to a world-wide competition, not only in the finished product, but in the wages of labor, the standard of living and every other item of cost. They propose also in order to destroy the trusts to put all trust-made articles on the free list. This was a provision in the Gorman-Wilson Tariff Bill, and had necessarily the result, if enforced, of destroying not only the trusts but the entire competing American industry.

The normal operation of a protective tariff and the proper competition among those who enjoy its benefits, is the reduction of the cost of production. The encouragement which the industry receives leads to the investment of capital in it, to the training of labor, to the exercise of the inventive faculty of which the American has so much, and in practically every case in which adequate protection has been given, the price of the article has fallen, the difference in the cost of producing the article abroad and here has been reduced, and the necessity for maintaining the tariff at the former rate has ceased. In the case of steel rails, for instance, we began their manufacture in 1867 with a duty of $75 per ton. The selling price was $166 per ton. Four times since then the duty has been reduced until now it is $7.84 per ton. The present price is $28. Last year we made over three million tons, and are selling them all over the world. Again, take tin plate. In the manufacture of this we were completely dependent upon foreign nations until, in the McKinley Bill, a duty of $2\frac{1}{5}$ cents per pound was put upon the plate and a domestic industry was begun. The duty is now $1\frac{1}{2}$ cents per pound. In 1906 we made 1,300,000,000 pounds, and the price is less than the price we paid to foreign countries.

In the last forty-eight years, we have been under a protective tariff except for four years during the second Cleveland Administration, when the Gorman-Wilson Tariff Bill was in force. The certainty that such a bill was to be passed so disturbed the business of the country as to produce a panic even before the Gorman-Wilson Bill was substituted for the McKinley Bill, and during the four years when the Gorman-Wilson Bill was given full operation, the disaster to the business interests of the country, to the farmer, and to the wage-earner was greater than ever in the history of the Government. It is impossible to attribute the conditions during that four years to any other influence than that of the tariff. Immediately upon the accession of the McKinley Administration, the Dingley Bill was passed, and under the operation of that Bill we have had twelve years of great prosperity.

The impulse given to investment was so great that our business plants were expanded too far. Liquid capital was exhausted. The large corporations found it impossible to borrow. In addition to this there came revelations as to the mismanagement of large corporations and the infidelity of trustees, together with the lawless methods of railroads and of great corporations engaged in interstate commerce. This led to more rigid regulation on the part of the Federal Government and to drastic and in many cases ill-advised legislation on the part of the States. All these things tended to frighten capital, and to withhold it from application to the railroads and those industries whose normal progress required good credit. A panic finally succeeded, due to over-investment, which has had but few of the symptoms of previous panics. Farmers were never more prosperous, their farm products never sold at a higher price. Business is slowly resuming.

All that is necessary, therefore, to restore a prosperous condition is to restore confidence. The moral awakening of the people, due to the revelations, has made much more rigid and correct railroad methods and business methods; the injustice and confiscatory character of some State legislation has been corrected by the courts; the investing public are beginning to feel that business conducted on legitimate lines have nothing to fear, and we are just on the threshold of a resumption of good business if the confidence continues to grow.

It hardly needs any argument to demonstrate that the introduction into power of Mr. Bryan's party, with Mr. Bryan at its head, determined to put in operation a tariff which shall not protect the industries of the country, but which shall be adjusted for the purpose of securing the most revenue, must delay the restoration of confidence and must therefore obstruct the return of prosperity. It is true that Mr. Bryan proposes that the change and transition from the protective system to a revenue tariff system shall be gradual, but this is left to the indefinite discretion of the Democratic party, should it be put in power, and the length of the step, the extent of the change, is wholly uncertain and is impossible to define, and some industries must certainly be injured in this gradual change. As Governor Hughes of New York has said, the proposition means a series of tariff tinkerings which cannot but keep the entire business community in a constant agitation and alarm at the changes which are to be made.

The business community have knowledge that the changes to be made by the Republican party will be made on the principle that no domestic industry will be injured or destroyed by the reduction in the tariff. They do not know this with the Democratic changes, but are advised that necessarily some of the industries each time the tariff is changed toward a revenue business must be sacrificed to carry out the principle. If the history of the tariff has shown anything it is that the threat of a revenue tariff in a business community dependent on a protective tariff means business disaster.

But it is asked, Why is it necessary to change the Dingley tariff? The Dingley tariff has been in operation now more than ten years. That is a period longer, I think, than the operation of any other protective tariff that we have had. It is intended under the protective system by judicious encouragement to build up industries as the natural conditions of the country justify to a point where they can stand alone and fight their own battles in the competition of the world. Improved machinery and training due to our inventive genius, together with an extending home market, certainly reduce the cost of production. Treasury and court decisions have given constructions to the tariff different from those intended by its authors. There are many articles in common use today which were unknown when the Dingley Tariff Bill was enacted. Conditions with respect to the cost of articles abroad have changed just as they have changed in this country, so that the difference between the cost of production at home and abroad ten years ago was in many instances different and less than it is today.

I shall not stop to give the statistics of the enormous growth of the industries of this country under the Dingley Bill, the increase in the exportation of manufactures and of farm products, the steady increase in the wages of labor, the increase in the savings bank deposits, the improvement in the standard of living among the wage-earners. It is said, and truly said, that the cost of living has increased. So it has, but that, too, is ordinarily an accompaniment of good times. The question is whether the cost of labor has increased more than the cost of living, and until the panic came in 1907, there is not the slightest doubt, for the statistics show it beyond question, that the percentage advance in wages was very considerably greater than the percentage advance in the cost of living. The truth is that when we had the lowest prices in farm products and in all the other things that enter into the cost of living, we had the lowest price in wages, and there was greater suffering, and a greater percentage of unemployed than ever in the history of the country. Wheat went down to 50 cents a bushel, corn to 21 cents a bushel, and oats to 18 cents a bushel, while potatoes went down to 27 cents a bushel. The farmers were in debt, the mortgages were being foreclosed, and their condition was truly deplorable. Now they are prosperous, their products are selling at a high rate, their market is a good one, and this is all under the protective tariff. The classes in the community that are suffering are the business men and the wage-earners, and what they are suffering from is a lack of capital. This they can secure by a restoration of confidence.

Much criticism has been made of the Dingley tariff and the operation of business under it, because of the fact that in some of the protected industries the product is sold abroad and in foreign markets at a lower price than that at which it is sold here. At first this seems a conclusive argument to show that the tariff is too high and that the manufacturer is deriving a greater benefit than he should on the proper principle of the protective system; but then we learn that it is a common practice in free trade countries, as well as in protection countries, to sell at lower prices abroad than at home, and that this is due to a desire to dispose in bulk of a surplus product, or to the competition in a new field of trade and to the desire to keep up the business organization and maintain a going concern even when the product sold abroad is sold without profit, or even at less than cost. Still it must be admitted that such a practice, if it is constant through all seasons, suggests that the tariff may be properly reduced, and that the tariff is greater than the difference between the cost of production at home and abroad, and that it should therefore be reduced.

Mr. Bryan is concerned because he thinks that the Republican party is unable to carry out its promise of revising the tariff in accordance with the principle stated. He says that the protected interests are so necessary to the success of the Republican party that they will control it and prevent a revision on proper lines, and that there has been no indication that the revision may not be upward rather than downward. Mr. Bryan expresses the fear that contributions to the campaign fund of the Republican party will be so extensive from the protected interests that the party will be unable to rise above those interests in the formation of the tariff, and will, therefore, control it, to the exclusion of the interests of the consumer. I deny this. In the first place, I am able to say, on information of a somewhat accurate character, that the Republican campaign fund from every source is not now and is not to be large enough to debauch or demoralize any party, much less the people and the Congressional Representatives of that party. In the second place, the formation of a protective tariff is not the only kind of a tariff that is affected by persons having a pecuniary interest in its operation. A revenue tariff may be varied to suit certain parts and to operate as a protection for some people, and in the Gorman-Wilson Tariff Bill we had the example of how a revenue tariff bill could be framed with a view to protecting certain parts of the country, and leaving unprotected the business in other parts.

In response to Mr. Bryan's fears, I wish to say that the Republican party in its platform is pledged to a genuine revision, and as the temporary head of that party, and President of the United States, if it be successful in November, I expect to use all the influence that I have by calling immediately a special session and by recommendation to Congress, to secure a genuine and honest revision of the tariff in accordance with the principle of protection laid down in the platform, based upon the examination of appropriate evidence and impartial as between the consumer and the manufacturer. I do not for a moment dispute that the protected manufacturers will make every effort, as they ought, to maintain tariff at such a rate as will secure them in their business, and that in this matter they will be interested parties; but there is also a large element in the Republican party representing the consumer, through whom the demand for a revision of the tariff on conservative protective lines to reduce excessive rates has crystallized into the definite pledge to revise the tariff. This element too should be given a hearing.

The rank and file of the Republican party are in favor of this revision, but insist that it shall be in accordance with the time-proven policy of the party of protection. Under these circumstances, there can be no doubt that the representatives elected by the party will come to Congress imbued with the necessity for honorably and strictly carrying out the plighted faith of the party to make a new tariff on the principle stated.

The Republican party has given in the past seven years of the present administration an example of how it can rise above corporate influence, and has enacted laws and directed an executive policy that were bitterly resisted by the many corporations affected. The moral awakening which took form under Theodore Roosevelt continues today and is gaining strength, not only in the country at large, but with the leaders and the rank and file of the Republican party. I have every reason to believe that the returning Congress, if it be Republican, will come there anxious and earnest to treat the tariff question fairly and energetically, but with a due regard to the maintenance of the protection principles on the one hand and to the interests of the consuming public on the other.

It is my judgment, as it is that of many Republicans, that there are many schedules of the tariff, in which the rates are excessive, and there are a few in which the rates are not sufficient to fill the measure of conservative protection. It is my judgment that a revision of the tariff in accordance with the pledge of the Republican platform will be on the whole a substantial revision downward, though there probably will be a few exceptions in this regard. As the temporary leader of the party, I do not hesitate to say with all the emphasis of which I am capable that if the party is given the mandate of power in November, it will perform its promises in good faith.

10

Postal Savings Banks and the Guaranty of Bank Deposits

Delivered at St. Paul, Minnesota, September 28, 1908

Fellow-citizens:

I wish to call your attention today to a plank in the Republican platform and to a plank in the Democratic platform which involve important though not controlling issues in this campaign.

Postal Savings Banks

I refer first to the plank in the Republican platform that recommends the adoption of postal savings banks. The Republican Convention doubtless had in mind the bill which had been introduced in the Senate and reported by the Senate Committee for passage, authorizing and directing the Postmaster-General to receive savings deposits at every money-order office, and at such other offices as he may designate, in sums of $1.00 or more, and multiples of ten cents after the first dollar. The bill provides that no one may deposit more than $200 in a month, and no one may have more than one account; that no one shall deposit in total more than $1,000 and that the interest which the Postmaster-General is required to pay on deposits, at the rate of 2 percent per annum, payable quarterly, shall not be paid on a larger deposit than $500 to any one person. The bill further provides that the money deposited shall be invested by the Postmaster-General, with the assistance of the Attorney-General and the Secretary of the Treasury, in a national bank in the same place in which is the money-order office at which the deposit is received, and that if there be no national bank at that place, then in the national bank nearest to the office in the neighborhood. The provision is that not less than $2^{1}/_{4}$ percent shall be received as interest on such deposits from the national banks, and that if an investment of this sort becomes impracticable, then the three cabinet officers shall invest the money in the town, county or State bonds where the post-office is situated.

The objection has been made that this is paternalism and socialism and is introducing the Government into the banking business. The objection is without weight. The *laissez faire* school of political economists and the supporters of individualism in society have had their theories very much modified by practical demands of society, and the principle embodied in the modification may be stated as follows: That where a general service to the public cannot be well discharged by private enterprise, and can be very effectively and economically discharged by the Government, the Government should undertake it. The postal savings bank comes exactly within this principle. If there were savings banks in all the country as numerous and as easy of access as they are in Massachusetts, in the New England States and in New York, it might be said that the postal savings bank was an invasion of territory properly occupied by private enterprises, although even then it could be pointed out, as the experience in other countries shows, that the function performed by the postal savings banks is much more comprehensive than that of the ordinary savings banks. But when it is considered that in only eleven of forty-five States are there savings bank facilities, when it is known that in the Middle West, east of the Rocky Mountains, the average distance from any post-office to a bank of any kind is thirty-three miles, and west of the Rockies is fifty-five miles, it readily can be understood that private enterprise does not supply the need of savings banks which, in order to furnish a motive and opportunity for thrift and saving, should be easy of access to the class whose welfare it is sought thereby to improve. Of the $3,500,000,000 deposits in savings banks, 33 percent is in New England, 38 percent in New York, 21 percent in Pennsylvania, Ohio, Illinois, Iowa and California, leaving but 8 percent of the total in other States.

The system was introduced first in England, in 1861, and has had unusual success. It was first proposed in 1807, and was vigorously condemned by all the banking interests, and it took more than fifty years to overcome the opposition. It was feared that it would injure the savings and other banks. Instead of this, it seems to have furnished an opportunity for the deposit of savings that found their way to no bank at all, and today the amount of deposits in the postal savings banks of England is $600,000,000, with an average deposit of $75. Similar systems have been introduced in France and Austria and most of the European countries except Germany, where they have a system of municipal savings banks that supplies the place of the postal savings banks. In all the English colonial possessions, the postal savings banks have been introduced, and I am glad to say that we have introduced it also in the Philippines, and that it is slowly making successful headway there.

We should not deny to our people throughout the vast extent of thirty-five States opportunity to make the small deposits with the security of the Government's promise to pay principal and interest. Such a system will add greatly to the money savings of the country. No private banking enterprise could possibly afford to establish savings banks throughout the thirty-five States where they have none, equal in number to the number of money order offices; and it has been demonstrated that the increase in the executive force of the post-office and the added cost due to the maintenance of such a system would be exceedingly small. These are all reasons for making it a Government matter.

The fear by any class of banks that this would interfere with their business the experience in other countries has shown to be utterly unfounded. Where savings banks are established they pay a higher rate of interest than the Government will pay for deposits in the postal savings banks, and confer privileges on their depositors which it would be impossible to grant under a Government system. It has been feared that the postal savings bank would gather up local capital and send it to Wall Street. Under the provisions of the law I have already stated, and in so far as it is practicable, the money would be retained in the neighborhood of the office in which it was deposited; but if the exigencies of business lead to its transfer by the depositaries to other parts of the country in search of greater profit, this is only the normal operation of business that would have a similar effect upon all capital deposited in banks, whether State or National.

I cannot conceive of a greater incentive to thrift among the people where it does not now exist than would be presented by the establishment of such savings banks. We have been slow in adopting a system which has commended itself so strongly to other countries by actual experience, and the need for which has been shown in this country in a peculiarly significant way. At many money-order post-offices, orders are drawn and the time for payment expires long before presentation, indicating that the drawer of the order merely put the money in the post-office for the purpose of depositing it, and not for the purpose of transferring it. In two cities in Montana the amount of such money orders in one year reached the sum of $300,000, and in other Western States a similar result was observed. Ninety-two millions of dollars were transmitted to European countries by wage-earners in this country, and there is reason to believe that a very large part of that money was deposited in savings banks abroad, and that had there been postal savings bank facilities in this country a good part of this enormous fund would have been retained here. The familiarity of the foreign immigrant with the postal savings system shows that it would be readily adopted here by him, and that much of the capital which goes abroad in this form would remain here for useful purposes.

A very significant fact in connection with the postal savings banks of the countries where they had been most successful, to show the money saved in addition to that now deposited in banks, is that one-third of the depositors of the postal savings banks abroad are miners and two-thirds of them are workingmen. This shows the useful function that such institutions conducted by the Government discharge.

The postal savings banks would perform a most useful function in case of panics because the fact that they are Government institutions with the whole credit of the Government behind them would attract the deposits of those small depositors whose runs in panic times upon the banks produce such disastrous consequences. The deposit of this money in Government offices and the power of the Government to re-deposit that money in the national banks in the neighborhood would furnish a means of meeting an exigency that no other system proposed has thus far offered.

Democratic Guaranty of Deposits

This postal savings bank system, however, does not meet the unqualified approval of the Democratic party. It has not the vote-catching quality and involves only the old-fashioned gradual movement toward better things by means of industry and thrift and saving. The party under its present leadership must have something which offers a short cut to reform at the cost of the honest and the industrious. The Democratic platform pledges the party to the support of a system by which all the national banks of the country are required to guarantee the deposits to the depositors in every bank, and this guarantee is to be performed by a tax upon each bank in proportion to its deposits, the proceeds of the tax to constitute a fund from which the depositors of any failing bank are to be paid; and if the amount of the tax is not sufficient to raise the fund required, then it is to be raised by subsequent assessment on all the banks of the country, and State banks are to be allowed to come in and get the benefit of the same guaranty under conditions to be imposed by law. While the Democratic platform does not elaborate the system, it is to be inferred from the fact that the precedent in Oklahoma is relied upon, that the provisions are to be like the Oklahoma law, and that those are as above stated.

No one can dispute the importance of making the deposits in every national bank as secure as possible, provided the remedy adopted is not itself worse than the evil to be cured. The Government has imposed certain limitations upon national banks which have greatly tended to reduce the losses of depositors. The first of these provisions is that every stockholder shall be responsible for the debts of the banks, after the assets and resources of the bank have been exhausted, in a sum equal to the par value of his stock. This is what is sometimes called the double liability of national bank stockholders. In addition to this, there are rules imposed by statute governing the investment of the assets of the bank. The bank is not permitted to invest in real estate. It may not receive more than 8 percent interest. It way not lend more than one-tenth of its capital to any director, and it is subject to periodical examinations by national bank examiners who are paid by the bank for the service rendered.

The result has been to introduce into national banks, a class of men of high character and great business and banking ability, and the losses in the last forty years to depositors in national banks have been reduced to an average annual loss of one twenty-sixth of 1 percent of total deposits. In other words, the national bank deposits are about $5,000,000,000, and the actual loss arising from failures of national banks does not exceed in the entire country, and in the more than 6,800 national banks, a total of $2,000,000. This seems a very small sum as compared with the deposits made, and shows a conservatism and care in the banking business that speaks well for the present system.

If the loss, even though small, could be avoided, it would undoubtedly be of great benefit and should be brought about, for while the percentage of loss is very small, the individuals upon whom the loss falls of course may be heavy sufferers. The question is whether we are to bring about an avoidance of this loss by the proposed Democratic remedy, or reach it in a more conservative and gradual way by perfecting the examination of banks, by rigid prosecution of all those who violate the banking laws, and by making certain rules laid down in the banking laws mandatory rather than directory, so that a violation of them shall subject the law-breaker to punishment.

Let us now analyze the remedy proposed by Mr. Bryan and the Democratic party. It certainly proposes to make the conservative banker pay for the negligence, carelessness, lack of confidence or dishonesty of the failing banker. It takes from one man without fault on his part money to pay for the default of another. That, I submit, is socialistic in the extreme, and so violates all equitable principles that the remedy should be condemned for this reason. If the fault or misfortune of one banker is to be paid for by his colleague who is without fault, there is not the slightest reason why all insurance companies, life and fire, should not be compelled to guarantee the losses of all companies, and it is difficult in principle to distinguish between such a proposition and a proposition that all the farmers of the country should guarantee each other's crops so as to save each farmer from the drought or blight that may come to his particular district in the vicissitudes of farming.

To say, as Mr. Bryan does, that the postal savings bank system is more socialistic than this is to give a very curious definition to socialism. Postal savings banks take no man's money to make up for the default of another. They merely use an arm of the Government, fully organized and well adapted to the purpose, to perform a much-needed business function which is not and cannot be discharged by private enterprises. Whereas the enforced guaranty plan takes out of one man's pocket engaged in the business of banking money to pay for another man's default. That is pure socialism.

Mr. Bryan suggests the expenses connected with the examination of banks is an imposition of a burden on one man for the default of another. There is no analogy whatever between the reasonable requirements for the examination of all banks and the taking out of one man's pocket money to pay for the ascertained fault of another. If there were but one banker and he a man of known probity and of the highest character, public policy would require an examination of his bank as thorough as that of any other bank. Trustees and public officers, no matter how pure their character or well-known their honesty, when they are subjected to the auditor's examination, have the burden on them to establish their honesty and correct business methods. So that it is entirely fallacious to assume that the provision for the examination of banks is a burden imposed upon the more conservative bankers in order to prevent dishonesty in the less conservative. It is a reasonable imposition upon all banks that their accounts should be examined, and that their methods of doing business should be constantly under public supervision, and it is reasoning, erroneous as it is refined, to make the pro rata cost of a general bank examination a precedent for taking money out of one man's pocket for another man's default.

Mr. Hill of Connecticut has shown that the effect of a guaranty law like the one proposed, if it had been in force in Connecticut during the last ten years, and the tax was only one-eighth of 1 percent, would have been the payment out of more than $4,000,000, and the receipt back of but $31,000. This illustrates the unjust, inequitable and socialistic character of a compulsory system most completely. The tax would, of course, ultimately fall on the depositors and not the stockholders—indeed, in the commoner forms of savings banks there are no stockholders; they are all depositors.

But let us pass the socialistic and inequitable feature of this system and come to the question whether it will really help matters. It is permissible under the national banking act for banks to organize with a capital of $25,000. The security which banks offer to depositors depends upon three things: first, the amount of capital; second, the amount of surplus accumulated from its earnings and kept on deposit in the bank and undistributed as dividends; and third, the personal confidence which the public has in the officers who manage the bank. Under the proposed system, a bank with a capital of $25,000 and no surplus, and with officers of little banking experience and with indifferent reputation, can offer to the public exactly the same security for the payment of deposits as a bank of half a million dollars, with $250,000 surplus, with officers known to be honest and able by thirty years' test. Depositors, therefore, in so far as the security of deposits is concerned, are just as likely to make their deposits in the $25,000 bank as in the bank with a half-million dollar capital.

It is proposed to introduce into the law a limitation as to the amount of interest which under the system can be offered and paid on deposits, and this, it is said, will prevent banks from offering excessive rates of interest to obtain deposits. What this limitation will be is not stated. In Oklahoma it is 3 percent. A limitation of this sort is very difficult to fix, because conditions vary so much in different parts of the country. That which would be high interest for deposits in one part of the country would be low in another, and that which would be high interest at one season and under existing monetary conditions would be low at another time. Hence, whatever limitation is imposed, except when the normal interest is highest, there must always be an opportunity for those inviting deposits to pay a higher rate than that which conservative bankers would pay.

The officers and stockholders of the $25,000 bank, therefore, are able to say to the depositing public: "Come and put your money in our bank. It is just as secure as the half-million dollar bank up the street; indeed, their assets are in fact security for our deposits. We will give you the highest rate of interest, and we will extend to you many other accommodations in the way of banking facilities and exchange. We will grant you loans when you need them, and we will do everything to make your stay in our bank comfortable. We shall not be too particular as to the security we exact." By use of leg muscle, by advertising, by pulling of many social and political strings which hang out for those who know in a community, it would be entirely possible for the enterprising officers of the $25,000 bank to secure as large deposits as those of the half-million dollar bank. This possibility suggests the motive for any band of speculators, desiring to promote some particular scheme, to organize a bank and obtain the credit which it is possible to obtain in the way described.

It is said that the larger capital will attract those who wish larger loans, but if by dint of using the means I have described the deposit of the bank is increased to half a million dollars, there is no reason why the accommodations of the $25,000 bank may not be as large as those of the half-million dollar bank. If the amount of the capital of the bank, the amount of the surplus, and the personal and banking character of the officials of a bank cease to operate as a motive for the public to make deposits with the bank, why may we not—indeed, why must we not—look for a complete change in the banking system of the country, for a reduction of the capital in banking, for a cutting down of all surplus, by the immediate distribution of dividends and by the withdrawal from such a system of all who find that neither capital nor character gives them advantage over bankers without either? It necessarily will level down the character of those engaged in banking. On the other hand, it will attract men of a speculative turn who, even if they are not dishonest, will exercise much less care than at present in respect to the character of their loans, because the risk of loss which they run, to wit, the loss of their stock, $25,000, is no such restraint upon them as bankers now have under a system in which the deposits are in some degree proportioned to the capital and surplus of the bank available for the payment of its creditors.

If the losses were limited to one twenty-sixth of 1 percent the amount of the tax on the deposit, of course, would be small, and each bank could readily pay it, although the principle would be an entire departure from equity; but the effect of the guaranty system on the character of banking would be such that the losses arising from stimulated recklessness would greatly increase, and the tax must increase to meet the losses on every bank in proportion. Instead of loss equal to one twenty-sixth of 1 percent annually it would rapidly increase in every financial stringency.

The history of the banking system in the State of New York furnishes a precedent of great significance in this matter. The Legislature authorized certain banks to issue currency and required them to contribute to what was called a safety fund, to secure their redemption. The contribution was 3 percent on the capital of the banks. The system worked satisfactorily until the court decided, to the great surprise of the State authorities and the banking community, that under the peculiar and unfortunate language of the statute the safety fund was liable not only for the circulating notes of the banks but also for their deposits. Within two years after the decision six banks failed. The safety fund was utterly insufficient to pay the losses. The law was then at once amended so as not to make the safety fund liable for deposits. Now, I am quite willing to admit that the New York case was not a test of the operation of the proposed system, so far as providing adequate security was concerned; but it is a most significant precedent in showing what the effect of such a guaranty of deposits is likely to have on bank management and the increase of losses. Mr. Knox, the standard authority on banking, says: "When it was found that all the debts of every description were to be paid from it (*i.e.,* the safety fund) a fictitious credit seems to have been given to the chartered institutions which was used by some of them in recklessly contracting debts for their managers." This is exactly what might have been expected and what may be expected in the proposed guaranty system. It gives to every banker, however inexperienced and reckless, and however small his capital, a credit without any adequate limitation or restraint, and is certain to lead to speculation and disaster in instances enough greatly to increase bank failures and losses.

Two objections are made to the conclusion that such an enforced guaranty system would lead to recklessness and disaster in banking. One is that the Government examinations would prevent, and the other is that it is an insult to the banking community to assume that the national bankers of this country, in view of their present high character, would yield to the temptation to recklessness presented by the system. I answer to the first objection that the Government examination does not prevent failing banks now; that it is quite difficult for a bank examiner to discover the unwise recklessness and speculative loans, and that often such loans are made between Government examinations, and then the evil is done and cannot be remedied by strict supervision. Government examination is a good thing, but where there would be such a temptation to recklessness it could not furnish a protection against it. Second, while I fully concede the general high character of the bankers throughout this country, my point is that the opportunity to obtain deposits and invest them on very little capital afforded by the guaranteed security will attract into the banking business men of no experience and of speculative tendencies and will distinctly lower the tone of the banking business.

It has been said by Mr. Bryan that the Republicans of the State of Kansas, by adopting a plank in favor of a kind of guaranty of deposits, rebuked me for my opposition to the plan outlined in the Democratic platform. This is entirely inaccurate. The Republicans of Kansas have recommended the passage of a law which is in effect an enabling act under which State banks are authorized to guarantee each other's deposits. That is, banks, if they choose, enter into an arrangement with other banks by which they shall all be subject to an assessment to pay the loss to the depositors in any bank in the agreement. It is the voluntary feature of the Kansas proposal that makes the radical difference between it and that of the Democratic platform. It is entirely conceivable that banks in the same neighborhood and within the observation of each other may profitably and safely accept and guarantee the security of all for the benefit of each, especially when they can select their partners. It is not necessary for me to approve or disapprove such a system. This is a national campaign, and the action of the State is not a proper subject for consideration or discussion. It is sufficient to meet the argument of Mr. Bryan to point out that the Kansas proposition is entirely different from that of the National Democratic platform, and that the arguments which I am attempting to state against the Democratic proposition do not have application to the Kansas plan.

One of the great merits claimed for the enforced guaranty of deposits is that it will prevent panics, and as panics frequently precipitate financial depression, it would be an excellent result. It is sufficient to say that the plan proposed cannot prevent panics. A panic is not stayed by the promise that money will ultimately be forthcoming. It can only be stayed by the production of the money itself. When a financial stringency is on, it is the cash the man needs, and to say that he will get it next week certainly does not assist him. No one who has heard that his bank was going to fail will delay in immediately applying for his money and drawing out his account merely because some time in the future he is assured that he will get it. Therefore, the system could not stay panics unless the fund were large enough to enable the banks run upon to pay all their depositors at the time of the run. Assuming that the banks have 25 percent reserve in their vaults, it would require to meet the obligations, therefore, 75 percent of all their deposits. Now, the tax is proportioned only to the loss sustained after liquidation and payment, so that the fund would be utterly inadequate to meet the demand for ready money which would prevent a panic. The total deposits of the national banks are $5,000,000,000. One-half of 1 percent upon that (and this is a much larger percentage than proposed) would make a fund of $25,000,000. The amount of money that was needed to stay the late panic in New York banks alone was many times this sum, so that it would be utterly inadequate. In other words, the cash needed to stay a panic, when the panic is on, it is impossible to accumulate in any other way except by such emergency measure as is provided in the Aldrich-Vreeland Bill, in which banks are given an opportunity upon proper security to issue $500,000,000 to meet such an emergency and are prevented from overissuing by the imposition of a heavy tax of 5 percent.

The proposed guaranty plan also invites the coöperation of State banks, and proposes that they shall have an opportunity to come into the same guaranty. The practical objections and difficulties do not frighten Mr. Bryan at all. He pays no attention to the difference that there is between State banks and national banks, or to the fact that State banks and trust companies and savings banks are all of them authorized to lend money on real estate, whereas the national banks are wholly prevented from so doing. The difference in the business and the tying up of assets between the systems is radical. It would be impossible to bring in the State banks without making the supervision of them quite as strict as of the national banks, and if that supervision is to be strict, it must be under national auspices; therefore they must in effect become national banks. This will entirely destroy the system of State banks, and will introduce trust companies and savings banks into the national banking system.

I am quite aware of the attractiveness of the proposition. I am quite aware that every one who has lost anything by a bank failure welcomes the suggestion of greater security and when the proposition is advanced he naturally seizes upon it with the avidity of one who has found what he seeks. The comparative smallness of the losses arising under the present system suggests to him how easy it is to meet those losses by a small tax upon the total deposits. He does not at first consider the general effect that it will have upon the character of banking and the necessary increase in the losses which will follow.

Mr. Bryan says that, as the Government has security for deposits in the banks, why should not the individual depositor have security. The Government's deposits are usually not a commercial matter, and they are usually passive deposits that are not checked out every day but are allowed to lie a long time in the banks. The Government is rich enough and strong enough not to give deposits to the bank if it does not choose to, and may keep them with entire security in a safe of its own. It only makes the deposits for the purpose of releasing the proceeds of taxes which are not immediately necessary for the use of the Government, and which it is in the public interest to have deposited, in order that the money may go back into trade; but as the Government generally makes nothing out of the loan, except the benefit to the public just stated, and as the Government would be greatly embarrassed by inability to secure its money when it needs it, and as the money is the money of all the people, the statutes require such security, and the advantage to the bank in getting the money and the prestige are such as to make it worth while for the bank to give security; but if a bank were required to give security for all its deposits, it would require the investment of all the capital in securities, and banking would cease to be attractive to any one. But the example of the security for deposits does not justify the proposed system, because the Government gets its security from the bank that receives the deposit. It does not get its security from all the other banks in the community, and they are not required to furnish security for that which they do not control or have custody of, which is the system proposed by the Democratic platform.

I think I have shown that the tendency of the system proposed would be to destroy the high character of the present banking system. This is not, however, to be taken as an argument that the security of deposits is not a good thing and is not to be brought about as fully and perfectly as possible. It is only to show that the method here suggested is a plausible but sophistical method that will not accomplish the purpose, but will ultimately increase the losses from bank failures.

The case of Oklahoma has been cited as an instance to justify the Democratic platform. The system has been in operation in Oklahoma only since March of this year. No panic or other financial disturbance has tested its efficiency. The statement is made that the public has so much confidence in the banks that the deposits in the unsecured banks are running down and the deposits in the secured banks are running up. If my correspondents in Oklahoma can be credited, this increase of deposits was due to the fact that $3,500,000 of the State money received from the Government for public school lands was removed from the national banks and put in the State banks operating under the guaranty, which would explain nearly all the increase in deposits. I do not think the matter important, however, for I am entirely willing to assume in the discussion that the promise of security of such a system would attract depositors. But it is interesting to note how the Democratic authorities of Oklahoma are anxious to make evidence in favor of the system by use of the State funds.

My information with respect to the Oklahoma system is that it is developing as might be expected. I have a correspondent who is intimately acquainted with the conditions in Oklahoma. In a letter of September 22, 1908, in speaking of the effect of the Guaranty of Deposits Law, he uses the following language:

"Conditions in Oklahoma are growing worse than was expected on account of the recent decision there whereby it was decided that the Bank Commissioner has no right to refuse to grant a charter to parties proposing to organize a bank. As an instance, in a town of less than 500 people as many as four banks have been organized. Application is now in for the organization of the fourth bank in one town of only 470 population.

"Men whose past records proved them to be incompetent are engaging in the banking business and getting in control of banking institutions. I have knowledge of one instance where a man was engaged in business some years ago and failed. He went to another town and engaged in the same line of business in his wife's name, but conducted her affairs in such an unbusinesslike way that she failed. Some time afterward he went to Oklahoma Territory and started a small State bank, but found he could not succeed and sold to other parties and left the territory. A few months ago, however, he returned and started another State bank, advertising that the depositors are secured under the State guaranty law, and after sixty days' operation he now has over $100,000 deposits. I have it from the best authority that he now proposes to start fifteen new State banks throughout the State, two of which have already been organized and one now doing business."

I began my address by describing the benefits to be derived from the postal savings bank system. This has the feature of a guaranty by the Government under circumstances which justify it, because it receives and husbands the deposits.

The guaranty will, of course, attract deposits, but the interest fund is so low that the usual customers of savings banks will not be drawn away, as experience in all other countries show. The Democratic platform proposes, if the guaranty system cannot be put in force, then to adopt the postal savings banks, as if the guaranty system supplied the needs met by the postal savings banks. This is entirely untrue. No enforced guaranty system will supply what the postal savings bank will supply.

11

Labor and the Writ of Injunction

Extract from an Address Delivered in the Auditorium,
Topeka, Kansas, October 3, 1908

It is said that I have decided against labor; that I have issued injunctions in labor suits. I have. I was a judge on the Bench, and according to old-fashioned notions when I was on the Bench—of course, since I have been running for the Presidency those notions may have faded out some—I was required by my oath to decide the case as the law and the evidence required, and to furnish to the man who was injured or threatened to be injured, all the remedies that the law justified me in giving him and that the law justified him in having, and when I issued an order in his favor that he was entitled to have, I saw to it that it was enforced, and anybody that got in the way of it got hurt, and I am not apologizing for that at all. But what I want to tell you about is those cases. I want to show you what is a fact; that, while it happened that generally in those cases I had to decide against the lawless workingmen who were attempting to do something that the law did not permit, I laid down the principle of law defining the rights of the workingmen and the corresponding rights of the employers, and that those principles obtain today and that they are the principles upon which the trades unions and labor organizations have built themselves up as lawful organizations within this community and have exercised the healthful and lawful influence that they do today.

Let us see what the first decision was: A boss bricklayer got into trouble with his men and they struck. They belonged to the Bricklayers' Union. The Bricklayers' Union notified every material man in Cincinnati that if he furnished any material to that boss bricklayer they would declare a boycott against him. Moores and Company were lime dealers. They went to the boss bricklayer, with whom they had a contract, and they said: "We don't want any trouble with the Bricklayers' Union. You have got a contract with us, but we would like to have you release it." He said: "All right, I will get my lime; you do what you please." The way he got his lime was to send a man down to the yard where there was a freight car from which Moores and Company sold lime to anybody that came for it. The walking delegate of the Bricklayers' Union saw this done. He reported it to the union and they declared a boycott against Moores and Company, the lime dealers, and broke up their business. Moores and Company brought suit against the Bricklayers' Union on the ground that this was an unlawful secondary boycott and they were entitled to recover damages. The case came before a jury. The jury rendered a verdict for $2,500 in favor of Moores and Company. The case came up to the general term where I sat with two other judges, and we decided, and I wrote the opinion, that a secondary boycott, by which a third person, not interested in the controversy, was drawn into it by one or the other and threatened by the boycott and thus made to come into the controversy by duress or to stay out under penalty of boycott, was tyrannous, un-American, un-Republican, was against common law and ought not to be the law and was not the law, and that the person who instituted the boycott was liable in damages to the person who suffered on account of it. The jury, as I say, returned a verdict, and it shows how full of efficacy such a remedy was in that Moores and Company have still upon their books that judgment for $2,500 without a cent recovered on it.

The next case: I didn't think I was going to be foolish enough to run for the Presidency when I was on the Bench. I don't know whether I could have avoided getting into these cases or not, but nothing ever happened in the way of a labor controversy within a hundred miles of me that I did not flounder into it; so that when the Toledo & Ann Arbor road got into a strike with the Brotherhood of Locomotive Engineers and it began to be rumored that the engineers of the Lake Shore would not haul the cars of the Toledo & Ann Arbor road, which was its chief connection, the Toledo & Ann Arbor road brought an injunction suit against the Lake Shore, in which they averred the intention of the Lake Shore to refuse to haul their cars, and not only against the Lake Shore road but against the officers and employees, and they got an injunction, commanding the Lake Shore, its officers and employees to haul those cars, and the employees were notified, the officers were notified and the corporation was notified. P. M. Arthur was the leading labor leader of those days. He was at the head of the Brotherhood of Locomotive Engineers—of course, in my judicial experience I had to run up against the biggest of them—that was my luck. They came to me to tell me, and showed it by affidavits and otherwise that P. M. Arthur had notified the engineers of the Lake Shore road that they were not to haul the cars of the Toledo & Ann Arbor road; and that in spite of the injunction that had been laid upon them and in spite of a specific statute of the United States that made it an offense punishable by fine and imprisonment for those employees, while on their engines and acting as employees, to refuse to haul those cars. I notified Mr. Arthur that he must withdraw his order to his engineers to obey that secret rule No. 12 not to haul those cars of the Toledo & Ann Arbor road. Mr. Arthur was a law-abiding citizen and he withdrew that order, the case was heard, the injunction against him was sustained and the engineers of the Lake Shore road continued to haul the cars. The Toledo & Ann Arbor strike went on and I do not know how it resulted.

Now, when that was done there was a tremendous outcry. I wrote the labor opinion. I don't think anybody read the opinion except possibly the reporters and some gentlemen who were seeking legal literature, but I do know that I was condemned by the railroad orders from one end of the country to the other for having done an act that was tyrannical and that was to revolutionize everything and enslave the railroad order men. I was talking the other day to a leader of one of the orders and he said just that to me, "but," he said, "we had this experience afterward. We got into a row with the Gould roads and Judge Adams of St. Louis issued an order of injunction preventing our chiefs from ordering us to strike or from negotiating on our behalf, on the ground that they had no right to interfere or advise, that sort of a thing." Well, that was a pretty broad injunction, one that could not be sustained, and they had the good sense to hire a good lawyer and to go into court and to ask Judge Adams to withdraw that injunction, and then the chiefs of the orders concluded that they would read my opinion, written some four or five years before, and to their surprise they found that I had there laid down the rights of railway and other labor organizations in such a way that the order of Judge Adams was entirely wrong, and that if he followed me as authority he must withdraw the injunction. They submitted that opinion to him, he examined it, and he withdrew his injunction, and they went ahead with the strike and won it. The same thing occurred just six months ago in Judge Thompson's court with the Typographical Union. In those cases I laid down this principle: that laboring men not only had the right but that they ought to unite in their own interest, in order that they should meet on a level with the more powerful capitalist employers; that they had the right to elect officers who should represent them in these industrial pursuits; that they had the right by assessment to accumulate funds in order to support those of their members who were in a strike; that they had the right to withdraw from association with their employers and to withdraw all their friends from such association, but that they did not have the right to injure their employer's property or to initiate against him a secondary boycott. I also laid down the rule that no injunction should issue to prevent a man from striking if he would, or all the men striking if they would, because that would be slavery. Those are the principles I laid down, and I say that upon those principles has been guided every labor organization since that time, and they have kept within the law. If you will read my opinion you will find the principles there stated.

12

The Debate of Lincoln and Douglass: A Look Backward

Delivered at Galesburg, Illinois, October 7, 1908

The debate between Mr. Lincoln and Judge Douglass, which took place at this spot, was one of seven historic discussions between them in Illinois. Neither speaker represented the extreme view of some of his party. The controversy related to the status of slavery in the territories of the United States and its succeeding status in States to be formed out of that territory. Judge Douglass's position was that the question whether slavery should be made lawful and should be protected in a territory was to be determined by the people resident in a territory. That was the doctrine of squatter sovereignty. The extremists among the pro-slavery advocates in the South maintained that it was the duty of Congress by legislation to protect slave property in the territories, and that to live, slavery must expand, and therefore that the admission of slave States must be favored rather than free States, and additional territory of the United States should be acquired for the purpose. Mr. Lincoln's position was that slavery was wrong, that a majority of those who framed the Constitution and founded the Government believed it to be wrong, and hoped for its gradual and ultimate extinction; but that pending this change, they provided for the protection of slaves as property in the Constitution by directing Congress to pass a fugitive slave law, and made it impossible for the Federal Government to abolish slavery in the States in which it was recognized as valid by law. Mr. Lincoln, therefore, while he deplored the existence of slavery, believed that as a sworn legislator it was his duty to vote to provide a fugitive slave law and such other protection to slave property as was required by the Constitution. He insisted, however, that slavery was wrong, and that it was the duty of Congress to forbid slavery in all territory of the United States where it did not exist. He pointed out that the founders of the Constitution and early legislators had demonstrated by Federal statutes which they enacted on the subject, that they believed Congress to have the power to forbid slavery in any of the territory of the United States, including the District of Columbia. The extreme party on the side of Mr. Lincoln were the abolitionists, who believed that slavery was wrong, who denied any obligation because they claimed it was an immoral one, to pass a fugitive slave law, and who relied upon the higher law as justifying a violation of the Constitution in so far as it made provision for the preservation of property in man.

We thus had, at the time of this dispute, four parties, the extreme Southern pro-slavery party, the squatter sovereignty party, the Republican party determined to oppose the extension of slavery, but willing to admit its legal status and the obligation to protect it as far as it existed, and the abolitionists who recognized no obligation to protect it at all. This peculiar condition in respect to the controversy led the contestants into a statement of nice distinctions which separated them from the extremists on their own side and relieved them from the embarrassment of their position.

Judge Douglass was not only a candidate for the Senate from Illinois, but he was a candidate for the Presidency. Mr. Lincoln put him questions which compelled him to make clear the difference between his view and that of the pro-slavery Southerner. As Mr. Lincoln anticipated, Judge Douglass lost forever the possibility of support by that ultra pro-slavery wing of his party. That was the most compact and unyielding faction of the Democracy. Judge Douglass's nomination for the Presidency by a united party therefore became impossible.

The abolitionists and extremists on Mr. Lincoln's side did not occupy the same position of influence in the Republican party as the extreme pro-slavery wing did in the Democratic party. Hence Mr. Lincoln's position of recognizing the obligation to give to slavery all the protection required by the Constitution and no more, while it angered the abolitionists did not seriously interfere with his becoming the Republican nominee. The acuteness and political foresight of Mr. Lincoln in this regard were shown by his prophecy that while the answers which Judge Douglass would make to his questions might reëlect him Senator from Illinois, it would defeat him for the Presidency. That is exactly what it did, and it did more, and probably Mr. Lincoln had that too in mind; for it not only defeated Judge Douglass for the Presidency, but it divided his party in such a way as to require two tickets and thus to make the election of the Republican candidate a certainty.

A reading of the debates marks a clear distinction between the two men. Judge Douglass was a masterful, fluent, forcible debater, not above resort to appeals to partisan prejudice and entirely willing to deny or ignore perfectly logical distinctions which Mr. Lincoln made in his statement of principles and of his position. Judge Douglass at times lost his temper, and resorted to epithet and denunciation. Mr. Lincoln never lost his temper and but rarely used a word of opprobrium which might better have been omitted. Much of the debate is taken up with a discussion of the record of each debater, and with an attempt to point out inconsistency between their present respective positions and those occupied by them in previous controversies in Congress and elsewhere. This is somewhat lacking in interest and presents a contrast to those parts of the debate that are devoted to a general discussion of the political and constitutional status of slavery, and to prophetic utterances as to its continuance or extinction which have an intense interest in the light of subsequent events.

It is perfectly clear that Mr. Lincoln had given years of thought to working out a consistent position with reference to the wrong of slavery. It was as revolting to him as to any abolitionist, but he was a lawyer and a statesman and a man of peace, and he recognized it as an evil which the founders of the Constitution had recognized in the same way, and he knew no course to pursue but that of abiding by the obligations of the Constitution and limiting the extension of the evil so far as that Constitution would permit. He and those with him must have suffered excruciating pain in the decision of the Dred Scott case which laid down the principle that Congress could pass no legislation interfering with the property in slaves in the territory of the United States, and the character of the decision by a divided court and placed on different grounds by the different judges doubtless justified him in his hope for a reversal if another case could be again presented. With the skill of the accomplished debater, while he protested against the correctness of the decision, he used it to embarrass his adversary by pointing out its logical consequence which was that if Congress could not forbid slavery in the territories, then the people acting under its authority could not forbid it.

This suited the extremists of the pro-slavery type, but it was the last thing which Judge Douglass was willing to admit, and therefore he was obliged to take what seemed an absurd position, that while Congress could not forbid slavery in the United States territory, the people of the territory themselves might avoid the passing of laws to protect it, and thus avoid the Constitutional obligation by its evasive violation. This did not strengthen Judge Douglass's position.

The circumstances focused the attention of the country upon this debate in Illinois and gave it supremely national importance. Slavery was the issue upon which had centered for fifty years all other political controversies, and now there was fought out, as in an arena, with the people of the entire country as onlookers, this discussion. Lincoln put into the debate his whole heart and soul and mind. He had reasoned with himself since his appearance in Congress in '46, where he supported the bill to abolish slavery in the District of Columbia, and he had a clearly defined position in his mind on all the questions arising out of slavery. No man in the entire country could have been selected so well calculated to meet, with the clearest logical force, with apt illustration and with an earnestness and convincing honesty of statement, the representative of the Democracy on these issues. It is not too much to say that Lincoln in his discussion settled the attitude of the Republican party, that his debates made the platform, and that, although down to the time of the debate he was by no means prominent in a national way or the foremost man in his party, he then became so by the demonstration of his fitness to lead in the part which he took in the debate. It is true that in subsequent speeches, notably the Cooper Union speech and the others which he delivered in the East, he clinched and drove home the popular impression of his greatness as a political leader and debater, but it was in the actual heat of the controversy, when millions hung upon the words of each contestant, that his nomination for the Presidency became a probable and natural result. In this debate, of course, no one whispered the probability of war or conflict between sections. Each champion disclaimed the slightest sympathy with violent methods or the pursuit of any other method than that purely within the law, and while Lincoln expressed the hope that slavery might ultimately be extinguished, he pointed to no method by which this might be accomplished, and did not even favor it as a policy with respect to the District of Columbia, where he contended that the United States had complete control. He was as much opposed to the bitterness of feeling growing out of the question of slavery as were the supporters of the other side, who constantly complained of the agitation, but he set his face like flint, and in this he had the Republican party behind him, against the acquisition of any new territory or the bringing into the Union as slave States of any States in which slavery did not then exist. He said slavery must be kept where it was.

The debate clarified the minds of many people and drew the issues more sharply than ever on the advance or retrogression of slavery. It was an epoch-making event, and brought about the election of Lincoln, the War, and all that followed. It is exceedingly appropriate that the fiftieth anniversary of this series of debates should be celebrated in fitting manner, for it is doubtful if any purely unofficial function ever had such important historical consequences attaching to it as this campaign for the Senate.

A study of the debates is also a study of the character of Lincoln, and one cannot leave the subject without attempting to point out the great qualities of the greatest American, the most typical of his kind.

Lincoln's origin was humble, and so affected by the poverty and straitened circumstances of his parents as to be almost miserable. His father was a rolling stone, illiterate and unstable. His mother, Nancy Hanks, died in Lincoln's youth, and he was brought up by his stepmother, who taught his father and himself to read and write. The privations of his early life it is hard to credit as we read a description of them. His mother must have been a woman of strength of mind and character—nothing else explains the development of Lincoln. The chief application of his life was the ascertainment of truth, the determination of a basis of right on which to build his conclusions with respect to life and business and politics. His mind was strongly analytical and in every issue which he had to solve, he was straining to reduce the propositions as they were advanced to their lowest terms, in order that by comparison he might settle the weight of each. He loved stories—he had a wonderful memory for them—but the inexorable logic of his mind did not permit him to use any story or any illustration that was not apt to explain and make clear his meaning. His mind was not a mind given to partisan advocacy. He would have made a great judge. His method of stating his case in an argument was fair and with none of the cheaper arts of the stump speaker. His style, reflecting his method of reasoning and the simplicity of the propositions to which he wished to reduce everything, was clear, lucid, forcible, but simple. It is impossible to read the debates between him and Douglass without noting the difference in the judicial quality of the two, and without having it impressed upon one that the strength of Lincoln's arguments was in the fairness with which he stated his opponent's position and the candor with which he dealt with points in respect to which he had a doubt. He united in a most wonderful way a shrewdness and skill in the presentation of his position with a judicial consideration of the arguments of the other side that has hardly been equaled among our great debaters. The strength of his argument, of course, and the earnestness with which he pressed it were intensified by the moral foundation upon which he stood. Slavery was wrong and freedom was right, but slavery was a necessary evil which had come for historic reasons and which we must deal with and keep within its present limits.

It seems to me, as I study the life of Lincoln, that there is more inspiration in his development and the position that he attained of heroism and usefulness to the country than in the life of any other one man in history. He had his weaknesses like others. His education was faulty. His ambition for political preferment was strong, and he sometimes avoided expressions of his real opinion at times when they might have injured his political career, but with the sure development of a moral issue of slavery, the part which he took in it, his character and intellect seemed to grow with the intense earnestness that the controversy developed. By a certain sort of intellectual discipline, by self-education, he clarified his methods of thought and expression so that he was able to meet every problem presented in the controversy by a solution as simple as it was effective. He was as hard with himself in testing by the fullest logic the correctness of his conclusions as he was with his antagonists. The hardships of his early life, his association with all sorts of people, made him understand the motives and the limitations of the plain people as no other public man of our period. He had a zest for politics and with his understanding of human motives he was able generally to checkmate his antagonist without an open rupture. The responsibility which he had to assume when he came to the Presidency was awful to contemplate, and the proverbial sadness of his features it is easy to understand. The criticism and abuse to which he was subjected in the crises of the Civil War it makes one ashamed to review as a matter of history. And yet it is of the utmost value in the encouragement of others engaged in the public service that they may not be borne down by the weight of hostile and persistent criticism in their efforts to serve their country with an eye single to the public interest. Mr. Lincoln's biographer and partner, Judge Herndon, raises a question as to whether love made up a part of Lincoln's nature. He suggests that his consideration and charity resulted rather from his sense of justice which compelled fair treatment of every one and made him considerate to every one, and that his charitable attitude of mind was rather the result of reasoning from the basis of right than from the soft heart. I do not know that such a discussion is profitable. Certain it is that we never have had a man in public life whose sense of duty was stronger, whose bearing toward those with whom he came in contact, whether his friends or political opponents, was characterized by a greater sense of fairness than Abraham Lincoln.

We have never had a man in public life who took upon himself uncomplainingly the woes of the nation and suffered in his soul from the weight of them as he did. We have never had a man in our history who had such a mixture of far-sightedness, understanding of people, common sense, high sense of duty, power of inexorable logic and confidence in the goodness of God in working out a righteous result, as this great product of the soil of our country. One cannot read of him without loving him. One cannot think of his struggles, of his life and its tragic end, without weeping. One cannot study his efforts, his conscience, his heroism, and his patriotism and the burdens of bitter attack and calumny under which he suffered, and think of the place he now occupies in the history of this country, without a moral inspiration of the most stirring and intense character.

13

The Solid South and Its Political Past

Delivered at Chattanooga, Tennessee, October 16, 1908

Ladies and Gentlemen:

It is very gratifying to meet such an intelligent audience so early in the morning. There are especial reasons why I am glad to meet the people of Chattanooga. From my earliest boyhood I can recollect the interest that my father took in trying to bring about the construction of a railway which should unite the North and the South by a line from Cincinnati to Chattanooga. He was one of the trustees engaged in the construction of that work, and he was the counsel engaged in defending the constitutionality of the act by which Cincinnati was able to spend $20,000,000 in order to make this iron bond between the North and the South. Subsequently it fell to my lot, first as a Judge of the Superior Court, to appoint Cincinnati Southern trustees, and subsequently for seven years as a Judge upon the Bench, to exercise control over the receiver that had charge of the railroad. Therefore, I can not feel as if Chattanooga were very far south. I can not feel as if it were very far from Cincinnati, and I do not feel, therefore, a stranger with the people here, although I happened to be in the city of Chattanooga very little.

Then there is another reason why Chattanooga interests me greatly; that is, that with the assistance of your Congressmen, with the assistance of your business men, with the assistance of those interested in this part of the country, we have been trying to induce Congress to buy a large tract of land between here and Chickamauga which shall be used as a great army post. We want 50,000 or 60,000 acres, and if we can only make Congress a little liberal, we can do a great thing for the army on the one hand, and, incidentally, possibly to some people of Chattanooga on the other.

Now, my friends, it was my good fortune for six or eight years to exercise the jurisdiction of United States Circuit Judge in a circuit that included Michigan and Ohio on one side of the Ohio River, and Kentucky and Tennessee on the other side, and during that time I had to visit and become acquainted with the lawyers of both sections. I had to become more or less aware of the conditions that prevailed in the four States and to compare them. No one need tell me that the only danger there arose to me from my association with the South and the exercise of jurisdiction therein was that of over-hospitality. There was something about my appearance that suggested the propriety of a dinner every time I came. The only reason I dreaded coming down here was the excess of hospitality. The warmth of feeling, the cordial reception that I had, awakened in me a deep sympathy and a great admiration for this Southern country, and an earnest desire to put myself as far as I could in the place of the Southern men and women and understand them, and understand their point of view. Hence it is that I am here.

When I knew you before, I was engaged in the respectable business of trying to administer justice. I have fallen from that state now, and am engaged in running for the Presidency; and it seemed to me that with the interest I have always had in the South, it was only proper that I should come here, and as a candidate for the Presidency on the Republican ticket express, by my presence and by what I might say here, my interest in bringing about such a result as will more closely unite the two sections than they have been united. It is quite possible that we may not get a single electoral vote in the South. I think we will get enough without it; but nothing would gratify me more than if I could enter the Presidential chair with the feeling that in the electoral vote that put me there were the votes of Tennessee and

Kentucky. We all know the history of the country, and we know the natural results of the War. We know how the South was ranged on the side of the Democratic party. We know its natural conservative tendency. We know the homogeneous character of its people, the preservation of traditions in the family. Why, I remember when I went to Nashville, Tennessee, and got into the families of some of the lawyers there, they were telling and enjoying the jokes, the forensic jokes and repartees and forcible arguments that had been uttered fifty, sixty and seventy years ago by the leaders of the bar. That would not be possible north of the Ohio River, because we have changed so that our family recollections do not go back that far. So it is entirely natural that even after all reasons have disappeared, the intelligent Southern people should vote the Democratic ticket and go on voting it just to preserve the historic traditions. I am here to see if we cannot make a beginning of disturbing that tradition and relegating it to the place where useless traditions ought to be.

The enormous industrial expansion of the South which has taken place since 1895, and largely under the auspices of Republican administration ought, it seems to me, to demonstrate to the thoughtful men of the South that their logical position is in the party which makes such prosperity possible. Right here in the centre of the manufacturing industries of the South, does it need an argument to convince you that the protective system is absolutely necessary to the continuance and maintenance of your prosperity? I know how that thing is adjusted. The Congressmen that represent each district are in favor of free trade for every other State but they are in favor of protection for this particular spot. A Democratic Congressman down in the southwestern part of Missouri feels that they need a little protection for zinc and is in favor of the protection of zinc against Mexico, but for free trade in everything else. I think you ought to come over to the party that is in favor of distributing the favors of protection all over the country in order to maintain all the industries of the country as they have been maintained on the system of protection. There are a great many men in the South, and doubtless many within the sound of my voice, who are strictly Democrats. They are to be divided into three classes. The first class are going to vote for me. The second class are not going to vote at all. And the third class are going to vote for my opponent and hope that I will be elected. I think, my friends, that you know, as I know, that that is a fair statement. So, I have come here to see if I cannot convince the two latter classes that what they ought to do is to come right out and just take their first cold bath in leaving historic tradition that naturally is dear to their hearts and come right into the party whose principles they approve.

I should like to go into some of the other issues of the campaign. One of the things that brought the North and the South closely together was the Spanish War. There, for the first time after the Civil War, we were able to demonstrate how close our hearts were across the Ohio River and the Mason and Dixon line by a rush to uphold the flag of our country in freeing Cuba and in maintaining the authority of that flag the country over. Perhaps I have misconstrued the people of the South, but my feeling always has been that the sympathies and the interest of the South were largely with the Republican policy in regard to Cuba, in regard to Porto Rico and in regard to the Philippines. My personal experience in the Philippines makes me think that there was as great an interest in the success of that experiment in the South as there was in the North. It is true that there was a good deal of eloquence hurled at us from the floor of the Senate and from the floor of the House as to the awful things we were doing in the Philippines and the liberty we were sacrificing, but when we called upon the South to furnish her quota of men who were to fight the country's battles over there, who were to make part of the efficient government over there, we did not find the South wanting, and I am glad to be able to say that in the service of the Philippines and in the selection of men to represent America there in that government we never paid the slightest heed to State lines. We have as many Democrats in the Philippine service today as we have Republicans, and we have as many Southern men as we have Northern men. Your own General Wright of Tennessee was Governor and made a fine Governor there. The present Governor Smith is a Democrat from California. Governor Ide and I are on the other side and are Republicans, but we did not know any difference out there and the pleasure of dealing with a government in which there was no difference and in which no sectional lines were recognized is what makes me long for a similar condition in this country.

I am not going this morning, into a discussion of the tariff other than to say what I have already said with respect to it. I feel certain that the business men of the South, certainly a great majority of them, had no sympathy at all with the free coinage of silver idea which was upheld by the Democratic party in 1896 and 1900. Certainly they haven't any now. I feel certain that Theodore Roosevelt by his courageous attitude with respect to corporations and corporation abuses has won the confidence and won the approval of the South, Democrats and Republicans, and now the question arises, What are you going to do in the South in this next election? Are you going to vote the same way that you have heretofore, and pray for Republican success, or are you going to assume some sort of responsibility with reference to the National government? [Voice: "Vote for Taft!"] That is an interruption that somehow doesn't ruffle me.

Senator Daniels and Senator Bacon, both distinguished Senators on the floor of that body, deplored the fact that the South has had no influence in the last twenty or thirty years in the councils of the Government. Well, I think that is true, and I join with them in deploring it, but perhaps we might differ as to the reason for it. I think it can be demonstrated that the reason for it is that heretofore the South has insisted on voting one way and praying the other, and then making itself an instrument of the Northern Democracy, no matter to what excess in economic doctrine that Democracy may go. They have been the tail of the Northern Democratic kite, and when you are carried in the pocket of a man and make no uncomfortable disturbance in that pocket you are not going to exercise very much influence with the gentleman that carries you. Furnishing no electoral votes and substantially but little Congressional support to a Republican administration, it is not human nature that your leading men should have influence with the Republican Administrations. What I am hopeful of is that these gentlemen who really sympathize with us will come over, will swell the present Republican party to a size that shall give us the electoral vote, and that then the Republicans of the South as Republicans shall come into the Administration and have that influence and power that the South is entitled to have by reason of her intelligence.

I want to close with a mere statement of a business proposition. We had a panic. We had a financial depression. I suppose it has reached you here. There are parts of the country to which it has not reached, in the West and among the farmers; but among the business men and the manufacturing men, the railroad men, both managers and laborers, the fact that we have had a panic is known. We are gradually struggling away from the financial depression that followed it. It came because we had got too far stretched out in our investment of capital, and the profits on it did not come in rapidly enough to furnish liquid capital to carry on the business of the country. There was a stringency. Then, too, the revelations with respect to corporate mismanagement, to lawlessness and threats of drastic legislation from the States, all frightened those who control the capital there was to invest, and nobody was able to borrow any money. The railroads of this country furnish a very large part of the demand for manufactured products. When they were utterly unable to buy, it so reduced the demand as to interfere with our great manufacturing interests, but our farmers were in a prosperous condition, everything was ready to resume prosperity if we could only get the money and the confidence with which to resume it, and that is the condition today. We are gradually forcing ourselves back to a level of prosperity equal to that we have had for ten years past. We are all in the same boat generally, whether we are business men, wage-earners, farmers or railroad men. We must have capital invested in order that the wheels shall go round, in order that the wage-earners shall be paid, in order that the farmers shall have a market in which they can sell their product. Therefore, we are all dependent upon the investment of capital. I know that proposition doesn't strike those gentlemen who follow Mr. Debs, because they don't believe in the institution of private property and they don't believe in having any capital at all, but just let the Government do it all; but we are rather more old-fashioned now, and we are depending upon the investment of money in business in order that business shall go on. We are therefore depending on the confidence that those who control investments shall have, and they live in Europe and they live in this country. They are those who control savings banks, and so control the capital of the humblest capitalist there is who deposits his money in the savings banks or other banks. Those men will not invest money unless they are sure of a business future, and the question I want to put to you is whether you think that by the installation of the Democratic party, under its present leadership, you are likely to restore confidence to anybody in the business future of this country. The gentleman who heads the party, after the disastrous years under the Gorman-Wilson Bill, recommended to us as a panacea and one that was going to help us out of the ditch in which we were, a plan which he called the free coinage of silver, but which ought to have been called the repudiation of 50 percent of our debts by statutory fiat.

Now, this was an alluring bait to farmers struggling under mortgages, an alluring bait to business men with their business prostrated. Just how it came to be so alluring to the wage-earning class, when it cut down their wages half in producing power, I never could understand, but the oratorical play and the poetic fancy reaches far, and there were many, even of that class, who favored the free coinage of silver. There was something tyrannical, there was something awful about the gold standard. "Protection," as the father of free coinage said, "protection has slain its thousands, but the gold standard has slain its tens of thousands." Now, that same gentleman, leading the Democratic party in 1900, although in that four years the fallacies of the theory had been laid bare and exposed, still brought forward that issue, a little bit shop-worn, and so he introduced another issue which was the paramount issue, of anti-imperialism, and he advised you and me that if he was not elected on that paramount issue liberty would depart from our hearts and we should not celebrate the Fourth of July any longer. Well, we may not have liberty in our hearts, but we have gone ahead celebrating the Fourth of July. Then, in 1904, he insisted on putting the same plank in the Democratic platform, but the Democratic party for the time revolted, and it didn't go in in any form. Then Mr. Roosevelt was denounced as subject to corporate influences and as being guilty of executive usurpation and as upholding militarism to a point where he was going around the world with a chip on his shoulder, waiting for some nation to tread on the tail of his coat and then we would have a fight. What happened in the next two years? Theodore Roosevelt exercised a greater substantial influence for peace in this world than had ever been exercised by any monarch or any chief ruler of the world before. He brought to an end the Russo-Japanese War; be brought to an end the Central American War; he helped Santo Domingo upon her feet so that the European nations could not interfere; he went into Cuba and saved Cuba from a revolution, and, as I say, he made a record for peace preservation that no other man in the world has ever made. Then corporate influences came forward, and if there has been a President in the history of the United States who has shown himself freer from control of those influences, who has taken by the throat the abuses of corporations, I don't know one equal to Theodore Roosevelt.

Mr. Bryan went around the world and his Democratic friends said (for they have been as severe with Mr. Bryan as those of us in the Republican party at times), with his observation of world nations he is coming home. We have heard in advance conservative statements from him, and he is coming home to be safe and sane. Mr. Bryan seemed to resent that statement. He thought it did him an injustice, and he proceeded to demonstrate that injustice that he had been done by advocating ownership of interstate railroads by the Central Government and of all the other railroads by the States.

Then he helped in the organization of the Oklahoma Constitution and presented that fearfully and wonderfully made instrument to the world as the greatest fundamental instrument that had ever been struck from the brain of man. I have not time to go into the wonderful intricacies of that instrument, but if you are interested in the labyrinthian thread that you have to follow in going through that Constitution I commend it to you as an evidence of what is possible for the leader of the Democracy to think.

Mr. Bryan's idea of dealing with the trusts is to stamp them out altogether. The idea of Mr. Roosevelt and of the Republican administration and of the Republican party is that they ought to be regulated so as to keep them within the law, but that when kept within the law they are a part of our great prosperity, that the wage fund supports millions of wage-earners, and no remedy ought to be adopted, such as that suggested by Mr. Bryan, by which we are going to destroy not only the guilty but wipe out the innocent as well.

Then we have another theory that is so characteristic of Mr. Bryan that I will refer to it for a moment. The tendency of Mr. Bryan's mind is toward a theory that addresses itself at once to the approval of an audience, not one that fits into the drafting of a statute to accomplish anything. What he proposes is that we should make all banks safe to depositors by requiring every honest banker, every safe and careful banker, to endorse the obligations of every banker that is not safe and that is not honest. That is the proposition. If there ever was a more socialistic proposition than that, I do not know it. It might well come from Mr. Debs, but how it can come from a conservative Democrat I do not understand. The effect of it, leaving out the injustice and the inequality of it, would be to drive out of the banking business every one who relies, in that business, upon his capital and his reputation for banking ability and banking conservatism. It is inevitable that that is the result. Indeed, it is so in Oklahoma already. I read a speech at the Bankers' Convention by a man who had looked into the matter, and he said they were organizing banks down there with a capital of $10,000, and that they were receiving deposits of $100,000; that any one could organize a bank, it didn't matter whether his credit was good or not, if he only exercised his leg muscles. He is a gentleman who, to use the colloquial expression, has the glad hand for everybody, and he says to the depositors: "Come in and put your money here. We will pay you a higher rate of interest, and if you need to borrow money we will not be particular about the security you give." "But," the depositor says, "you have only $10,000 capital." "Oh," he says, "that doesn't make any difference; this million dollar bank up here is security that you will get your deposits back." Now isn't that a Bryanesque arrangement?

I leave it to you if the putting in power of a gentleman with those economic theories that sound so well from the platform when put forth with the force of oratory he has, who is able to convince himself and persuade himself of the soundness of such fallacies, is going to restore the confidence that we need in order to bring back prosperity.

14

Party Plans and Principles

Delivered at Newark, New Jersey, October 19, 1908

Ladies and Gentlemen, Citizens of New Jersey:

It is a great pleasure for me to speak in Newark. I have a recollection of speaking in Newark a number of times, and I have always had a most cordial reception. To find so many Democrats and Republicans, for I suppose they are both here, up so early Monday morning, indicates an interest in the coming Presidential election that speaks well for the solution of the questions which we will have in November.

The issues are set out in a great many different ways, but it always has seemed to me from the beginning that the real issue was whether you think that the Republican party, by what it has done in the last twelve years, is entitled to your confidence, or whether it has done something that ought to put it out of power. That is not the only question either, because I concede that even if the Republican party had done something that made you feel a little angry at it, which of course I cannot admit, it is much to be preferred to the Democratic party under any circumstances, considering the history of that party during the last twelve or sixteen years and considering the peculiarities, to use no more offensive expression, of the leadership of that party.

The first thing that the Republican party did in the last twelve years entitling it to gratitude was to take a decided position in favor of the gold standard, and in the fight of '96, to carry government and business honesty forward and establish business on an honest basis. It is a short time to look back to an issue like that and find that there is nobody now willing to avow himself in favor of free silver, considering the bitter discussion that we had in '96 and in 1900. Then the Republican party substituted for the Gorman-Wilson Bill, under which we certainly had not had prosperity, the Dingley Bill, and under that our industries have thriven to a point making our prosperity in the last ten years greater than any other country in the history of the world.

Then we had to fight the Spanish War. We fought it promptly and well. That war brought upon us, as most wars do, very unexpected burdens. We had first to take up the question of Cuba, which was the cause of the war, and settle the government of that Island. We put the Cubans on their feet, as we supposed, and they staid there for three years, and then they fell on their knees, and we had to go and help them again onto their feet, and in February we expect to make them an independent people again.

Again in Porto Rico, that Island came over to us, a small rich island, with a million people, but an island that had labored with other West India islands in a prostration of agriculture and a general business suffering the recollection of which makes a million people rejoice every night and every day, and thank God that they are under the prosperity that the Stars and Stripes have given.

Then we took up the Philippines. That was the hardest problem of the sequelæ of the Spanish War that we had to solve, and at every point, except when we had the treaty of peace which put the Philippines on us, we met the bitter opposition of Mr. Bryan and the Democratic party. In spite of that opposition we have gone on, have given them a good government there and have given them an honest administration of justice. We imported one thousand American school-teachers who taught 7,000 Filipino teachers how to teach English, and today we have half a million Filipino school children reading, writing and reciting in English every morning.

We have given them a partial control over the central government, full control over the provincial government and full control over the municipal government, and they are striding on, teaching themselves by practice and by the aid of the American agents there, how gradually to build up a complete self-government. All these problems were new. We had to pioneer. The Executive frequently had not even the aid of Congress, but when Congress came on it stood by the Executive. There were problems that had not been solved in the platforms of the party, and I may stop to invite attention to the fact that when the American people select a party to exercise the responsibility of government, one of the things that it ought to take into consideration is the efficiency and cohesiveness of the party. The Republican party has a sense of governmental responsibility and therefore the members are willing to yield their individual opinions on non-essential matters in order that the Government may go on, and that explains the efficiency of the Republican party; whereas the Democratic party has no cohesion except that of opposition to the Republican party, and when they get into power their sense of responsibility is not strong enough to carry them on to a consistent, courageous, efficient policy.

Then we took up the Panama Canal, which, for four hundred years, since the time of Charles the Fifth, had been the subject of discussion. We made a treaty with Colombia, buying the right to build the canal, and then the Colombian Senate thought they could squeeze a few more millions out of us, and rejected the treaty. Then the Panamanians revolted and established a separate republic, and within due time, not too long, not too short, we recognized that republic, made a treaty with it, and acquired a proper dominion over the forty-mile strip ten miles wide through which we are now building that canal. Under the present Administration there has been an organization of the brains, the machinery and the hands in such a way that in the course of five or six years any one who knows about the work can promise you its completion so that your Navy will sail from the Caribbean Sea to the Pacific.

I mention these things—they are not spectacular—but I mention them for the purpose of showing you that the Republican party does things and in the long run the party that does things is the party that makes progress in the country.

In the enormous expansion of business, in the prosperity that seemed to overwhelm us and carry us all along in the hunt for the mighty dollar, abuses crept in, mismanagement of corporations was revealed, lawlessness on the part of railroads and other corporations, so that there was a quickening of the American conscience, and a demand that these evils should be remedied, and the Republican Administration through Theodore Roosevelt took hold of it. You would think from the statements of Mr. Bryan that no progress had been made in the country, but when you consider what has been done, when you consider what the real evil was, the progress that has been made to better business methods, to better railroad methods, seems remarkable and hard to believe. Through the instrumentality of rebates and unlawful discriminations great corporations have been able to build themselves into monopolies and to stifle competition. By the passage of the Rate Bill and by the awakening through the country of the determination to have equal laws and equal application of them, the railroads themselves, only too anxious to get out of the unlawful condition of business in which they found themselves, have abandoned rebates, have abandoned unlawful discriminations, and have taken away the chief instrumentality by which illegal trusts and monopolies have been maintained. The combination of capital is just as essential to our progress as the combination of the parts of a machine, and the fact that the capital is great and the number of plants needed are many is no reason for denouncing them as illegal unless they are used for an illegal purpose. The normal, legal purpose of such combination is to reduce the cost of production by inducing economy in the management of the capital. It is only when undue means are taken to stifle competition that they cross the line of legality and that they ought to be restrained and punished. Therefore, Mr. Roosevelt and the Republican Administration have directed their attention to prosecuting the exact evil, which is the attempt to monopolize. Mr. Bryan, on the other hand, proposes to take steps which shall destroy the entire business. He proposes that we shall abolish the tariff on what are called trust-made articles. The result of the abolition of rebates has been the establishment all over the country of independent competitors of these large corporations. If you are going to take off the tariff on trust-made articles you are going to destroy the trusts all right; there will be no difficulty about that, and you are going to throw out of employment the millions of men engaged as wage-earners in those great businesses, and you are also going to destroy the independent competitors of the trusts, for they are just as dependent on the tariff, indeed more so, than the trusts themselves. In other words, the proposition is like burning down the house, as the Chinaman did, to get roast pig.

Again, Mr. Bryan proposes to cut off the trusts as you cut a tree off, at 50 percent of its height. He is going to have an arrangement by which the production of every factory shall be limited to 50 percent of the total production in the country, and if that line is overstepped, then the man who oversteps it is to be sent to jail. I submit that this is an utterly impractical and destructive method. It is not the fact that a man makes 60 percent of a product that gives him control of the business; it is the question whether he gets undue advantage over his fellows in such a way as to stifle competition. If he takes contracts with his customers by which he gives them a rebate at the end of the year for exclusive privileges, or if he undersells them in one part of the country and sells at an exorbitant price at another part, that is an evidence of a desire to drive out competition and is an attempt to monopolize, and men who resort to those methods, or to secure rebates from the railroads, which is the chief method, are guilty of violating the Antitrust Law, and it is that evil that we, the Republican party, believe all efforts ought to be directed to stamp out, and that any indirect method by which you limit the amount of the output is not only unjust but impracticable, because you unite in your condemnation and punishment the innocent with the guilty. How is a man going to tell whether he manufactures 50 percent or more, and how is he going to separate his plant, because one plant may make 60 percent of one kind of article and 40 percent of another and 30 percent of another? How is he going to tell in advance what his competitors are going to do? In other words, when you come to embody the principle in a statute it fails utterly to work. It is only useful for platform and campaign and anti-election purposes. It won't work out in a statute.

We are going to revise the tariff, but the question is how it ought to be revised. The Republican party is in favor of and is pledged to a thorough and genuine revision of the tariff on a well-understood principle, and that is that every industry, every product of the farm, the mine or the factory in this country shall be protected against foreign competition by a customs duty equal to the difference in the cost of production here and the cost of production abroad. That includes three elements and perhaps more, but three certainly—the cost of material, the cost of labor and the manufacturer's profit or the interest on capital. You take those three elements abroad and add them and those three elements here and add them, and take the difference, and that measures what the customs duty ought to be.

The normal operation of a tariff by reason of the competition behind the tariff wall, by reason of the inventive genius of the Americans, by reason of the business ability of American business men, is actually to reduce the cost of production in this country and so naturally to reduce the price to the American people behind the tariff wall. That has been the history of the tariff, and so, the Dingley Bill having been in force ten or twelve years—longer, I think, than any other protective tariff in existence—the time has come, or so the Republican party believes, to reëxamine and reduce where reduction is necessary, and probably that will be in the majority of cases, because the normal operation will be to reduce the tariff so that it shall continue to be the difference between the cost of production abroad and the cost of production here, but so that no legitimate industry in this country shall suffer; and where peculiar circumstances have prevented that reduction in the cost of production here, there the tariff shall be revised and elevated, if need be, in order to make the same measure of protection. But, as I say, the general result will probably be a revision downward.

That is essential to the prosperity of New Jersey. If there is a State that is a hive of industry and is dependent on the tariff, it is the State of New Jersey. I want to ask the voters of New Jersey whether they prefer that system to the one proposed by Mr. Bryan and the Democratic party; that is, what he calls a gradual transition from the protective system to that of tariff for revenue only. A tariff for revenue only means that they propose to address their attention only to the collection of revenue. That means, even if they do it gradually, that they have got to cut off some industries that are now protected until they have cut them all off and reduced everything to a tariff for revenue only basis. I ask you what effect on the business of the country it is going to have to cut off part of the industries at one time and part at another and part at another, one leg today, one leg next year, an arm the following year, and so on? Will it not produce a lack of tranquillity in the business situation that will make prosperity absolutely impossible? But, Mr. Bryan says, of course you can try it and then if you do not like it at the end of two years, you can take it back. Of course you can do that, and that is perhaps what would happen, but why permit him to try it at all if you are satisfied with the other system and if, as the people of New Jersey know, their prosperity is largely dependent on the preservation of a system that the Republican party has maintained for forty-eight years? But, Mr. Bryan says, we are not going to have a real and honest revision. Well, if we are not, and the protected interests can prevent, why didn't they prevent it in the Chicago Convention? The truth is the whole Republican party had crystallized sentiment in favor of that revision. The whole Republican party is obliged to give an honest and thorough revision, and it will be made before the people at large, and when the Republican party pledges itself the Republican party can be trusted. But, it is said that the protected interests own the party by contributions to the campaign fund, and therefore that the Republican party does not dare give us an honest and thorough revision. Well, I am somewhat familiar with the total of the campaign fund, and I am able to advise every one that there is not enough there to debauch either a party of the people or a very small body of persons, and that if anybody is aching to contribute to something that needs support he has the opportunity by sending it to the campaign fund. It is not true. The Republican party in the last administration has shown itself able, after full deliberation and discussion, to pass any law in the face of any corporate opposition, when the law addresses itself to the justice and to the honor of the Republican party.

Now, I wanted to say something about labor. I cannot finish that subject in the time I have. I am only going to discuss the question of the business future of this country from the present standpoint. We are suffering from a panic. The tremendous prosperity that we had led us on to investments that did not bring back a fair return at once. Liquid capital became exhausted. There was a stringency the world around. It was impossible for the railroads that make the best single market for our manufactured products to borrow any money at all. Under those circumstances, with the demand reduced, manufactured products fell off, and the difficulty of obtaining money finally brought about a panic. I ought to add that, in addition to this gradual exhaustion of liquid capital, there came revelations as to business mismanagement in this country, as to the lawlessness of railroads, and then, on the other hand, a reactionary threat of drastic legislation in the States that frightened those who controlled the capital that might have been invested. The result was a panic. Then there came a financial depression, but it had certain peculiarities. It was a panic in spots. It was a depression in spots. You go west of the Mississippi River and talk to them about a panic, and they do not know what you are talking about. The farmers are in a condition of prosperity never before enjoyed. Their farm products are high, their crops are good, and they are in a condition of comfort. All that is necessary, therefore, to put us back on a good business basis, because we can gradually feel the uplift, we can gradually feel a return to better times, is the restoration of confidence to those persons who control the investment of money for new enterprises. Now that includes European investors; that includes American investors; it includes those trustees and financial agents that control money that has contributed to savings banks and other banks and trust companies, for we are all, those of us who save, in a sense capitalists. It means that we must restore confidence on their part as to the business future before we can assure ourselves of a return of prosperity.

Now, I am only going to occupy you long enough to point out that the last thing that you ought to do in order to restore that prosperity is to put in power the Democratic party with Mr. Bryan at its head, for I want to submit to you, if you had control of the investment of funds, and wanted to be sure of a fair return, would you take a gentleman who in times of business disaster, in '96, recommended as a panacea for every ill the adoption of a law permitting the free coinage of silver, which should by legislative fiat pay off our debts by fifty cents on the dollar? Would you take a man who was in favor of reducing wages by half under such a provision? Would you take a man who, after that had been demonstrated not to be the correct method, finally urged that if you retained the gold standard it would lead to disaster, and who in the four years of McKinley's administration was shown to be a false prophet, nevertheless forced into the Democratic platform, in 1900, an approval of the same document? Not only that, but introduced a paramount issue of anti-imperialism, and who said that unless he was elected on that paramount issue, patriotism and love of liberty would depart from the hearts of the people, and that we should not celebrate again the Fourth of July? Well, we have been celebrating it, and it seems to me that our hearts beat with the same throbs of love of liberty.

Then came on 1904, and he sought to put in the platform of 1904 an approval of the doctrine of free coinage of silver. Then he went around the world, and his Democratic friends in this neighborhood said, to use their own expression: "He has become safe and sane from an observation of the nations of the world." Mr. Bryan resented that imputation, and he proceeded to demonstrate its injustice by coming home and proposing— what? He, a Jeffersonian Democrat, proposed a centralization. He said that there was no solution of the railway problem except that the Government should buy all the interstate railways, and that the States should buy all the intrastate railways, a centralization of power which makes, it seems to me, any patriot and any friend of this country tremble at the thought of what power it might put in a man down at Washington controlling such an enormous amount of property.

In the course of his political life he approved the Oklahoma Constitution which had initiative and referendum from bottom to top, and was only a basis of the proposition on his part to have a national initiative and referendum, and in that constitution there was this provision, which he said was the greatest work that had ever been struck from the brain of man: that when a court had its authority defied, and an indirect contempt was committed, a jury should intervene before the punishment of the person committing the contempt. That has since been introduced into the Democratic platform, and I can't discuss what I regard as its pernicious effect in weakening the power of the courts, but they had one peculiar provision in that Constitution which sets out their view of things. They had a corporation commission which should get evidence from any corporation, railway or otherwise, in the State, and if the agents did not answer, then the corporation commission was to turn itself into a court and was to sentence to fine and imprisonment, or rather fine with the imprisonment necessarily following, any one who should refuse to answer. In other words, they were going to impose the power on an executive commission to punish for contempt without a jury, but when it came to a court they made the jury intervene between the order of the court and the court's enforcement of that order. I don't exaggerate. That occurs in the Constitution of Oklahoma, and it is a perfect zoological garden of Bryan ideas. But it attracted the attention of Mr. Bryan because of its novelties, I suppose, finally in this campaign.

In addition to the proposition of the destructive methods of dealing with these larger corporations, so-called trusts, to have them keep within the lawful lines—he has another panacea. Mr. Bryan is going to save us all from the loss of our deposits in banks, and how is he going to do it? Presumably by the Oklahoma plan, because he points to the Oklahoma plan as a vindication of the proposed remedy, and that is that when a bank fails in Oklahoma, its depositors are to be paid by assessment on all the other banks, and they are to create a fund of 1 percent to pay that off, and then if the fund is not large enough they are to keep on assessing until the debt is paid. Let us see how that works. Of course, the plausible side of it is this: The loss arising to depositors in national banks for the last forty years in this country does not exceed one twenty-sixth of 1 percent. The deposits amount to about five billions. That means about two millions a year loss; so Mr. Bryan says if you will only raise a fund a little larger than that by a small assessment on each bank you will prevent anybody from losing anything. Well, will you? If the loss would remain at that sum undoubtedly you would, but let us see how it works—and we have the testimony of gentlemen in Oklahoma as to just how it does work and how you might expect it to work. In Oklahoma they can have a bank with a capital of $10,000. In the United States it requires $25,000. But let us take the Oklahoma system. They say that men who have failed in banking have now come back to go into the business again. They have raised a fund of $10,000 by scraping around, then they go to their friends and neighbors, by political pull and otherwise, and they ask them to deposit money in their bank. "But," the answer is, "you have only got $10,000. Your reputation is not very good anyhow. You have got a cashier who is threatened with indictment for embezzlement"—that was an actual case—"and I don't propose to have my money in that bank." "But," the urgent and active banker says, "you don't seem to understand the operation of the new law. You know Robinson, the old skinflint banker up the street here; he has a capital of $500,000, with a surplus of $250,000, and he has the reputation that nobody can get any money out of him." "But what has that got to do with it?" "Why," he says, "don't you understand? The Robinson bank is responsible for my deposits." Well, that is so, that is just the system; I am not exaggerating it; I am stating it exactly. How long do you think Brother Robinson is going to stay in the banking business if his $250,000 surplus is responsible for the $100,000 deposits of this gentleman with the shady reputation that has established a bank with $10,000 capital? How long do you think he is going to keep his $500,000 in? Can't you see that the result of that is going to destroy the personnel of your banking fraternity? It is going to put into the banking business all the exploiters, all the speculative men, all the men of dishonesty, who desire to use somebody else's money for their own speculative purposes, and that is the last panacea that we have from Mr. Bryan.

I ask you, my friends, in all candor, if you had control of the capital of the country and wished to put it into business, would you venture it if you knew that a gentleman of such unstable economic theories, so easily fooled himself as to their virtue, were to be put into the Presidential chair?

15

Mr. Gompers, the Courts and Labor

Delivered at Cooper Union, New York, New York, October 28, 1908

Fellow-citizens:

I am glad to have an opportunity to come face to face with representatives of labor unions, and to discuss with them the issues which have been raised in this campaign in respect to the attitude that organized labor should occupy toward the two leading political parties.

In the first place, Mr. Samuel Gompers, at the head of the American Federation of Labor, has attempted to deliver the entire organized union labor vote, and possibly the unorganized labor vote, to Mr. Bryan as the leader of the Democracy, and if this grant and delivery were complete, perhaps it would be useless for me to address you on the subject. But I venture to assume that the laboring men of this country, and especially those who are organized, are too intelligent and far-sighted and too independent and courageous in thought to allow themselves to be delivered as political factors by any leader from one party to another. I assume that laborers, like other men, differ in their political principles, that there are Republican labor men and Democratic labor men, and that it is not too late, even after Mr. Gompers' action, to argue out the question which party should be supported upon ground appealing to reason.

The record of the Republican party in Congress in its limited jurisdiction has been most remarkable in the number of valuable statutes which have been enacted in the interest of labor: the Eight Hour Law, the Sixteen Hour Law, the Model Child Labor Law, the Interstate Railway Arbitration Act, the Interstate Railway Employers' Liability Act, the Government Employees' Compensation Act, the safety appliance acts, some two or three in number, the appropriation investigating the cause of mining disasters—are all especially directed to the interest of laborers employed either by the Government, by the interstate railways, or at work within the District of Columbia, in the exclusive jurisdiction of Congress. This is a record of which any party may well be proud, and it is a record in which the Democratic party has no part. Not a single line of labor legislation was put upon the Federal statute book during the encumbency of the Democratic administrations of eight years out of the last forty-eight. Under those circumstances, it is difficult to see how any judicial-minded person can attribute to the Democratic party that active sympathy with labor in doing things for its interest that entitles it to the support of labor. In their platforms and in their declarations they are full of sympathy for the laboring man, but in statutes passed, in work accomplished, their record is nothing.

But it is said that the attitude of the Republican party toward labor in the matter of injunctions in industrial disputes is hostile. The representatives of labor have contended that the power of injunctions has been sometimes abused, in that the injunctions preventing freedom of action in industrial disputes by striking employees and the officers of labor organizations have been much too wide in their scope. In a number of instances, this is true, and the Republican Convention, for the purpose of calling the attention of judges to the necessity for greater care in this matter, inserted a plank in the platform requiring that the best approved practice in the matter of injunctions should be embodied in a mandatory statute. Under this plank it is possible to adopt a statute which shall specify the few instances in which injunctions without notice can be issued, and which shall provide that injunctions issued without notice shall not last more than a certain and a short time, and thereafter shall cease to be operative unless meantime a hearing by both parties is had before the court. In this way it is thought that the abuses in the matter of injunctions of too wide scope can be avoided. I have been willing myself to provide that no injunctions should be issued without notice, but it was thought too drastic a reform to take away all remedy in certain cases where, unless injunctions could be issued without notice, no remedy would twist at all.

The Democratic platform resolved that injunctions ought not to issue in industrial disputes in cases in which they would not issue in other disputes. This plank is meaningless if read literally, because no one ever contended that the fact that a dispute was industrial was a ground for issuing an injunction in equity. If it was intended to mean more than this, then it is deceitful. We may infer from the recently issued circular by Mr. Samuel Gompers that it was intended to mean more than this, and that it was intended to accomplish the purposes declared in a bill introduced at Mr. Gompers' instance, and which he says embodies the demands of labor. This bill contains two sections; the first section forbids the issuing of an injunction in industrial disputes in all cases except where an injury to property is threatened, and it provides specifically that an injury to a man's business is not an injury to his property right. In other words, it forbids the issuing of injunctions to prevent the injury or destruction of a man's business. Mr. Gompers has contended that the rules of equity did not permit the issuing of injunction to protect a man's business from injury. He is utterly wrong in this contention, and the decision of the Supreme Court of the United States, and of all other courts of any standing in the community, is contrary to his position, and we may well submit to laymen whether a business built up by hard work, attention to customers, in which a good will has been earned such that it can be sold at auction, is not a right of property or pecuniary nature, such as ought to be protected by the usual remedies of law and equity. It is just as valuable and sacred as the ownership of a house, or of the stock of goods on the shelf, and to remove it from protection of an equity right in industrial disputes is class legislation of the most pernicious character. Of all things not beneficial to the laboring man is legislation which operates on him as a class and seeks to give him privilege or immunity that is not enjoyed by other members of the community, and that is exactly what this provision as interpreted by Mr. Gompers and as understood by Mr. Bryan is to mean when it is to be acted upon in the National Congress.

The President, in a very apt letter, has asked Mr. Bryan to state his position, whether the platform as he reads it does favor the position of Mr. Gompers as stated by him in his bill, or whether it means nothing, as it would seem to mean when literally read. We have as yet had no answer from Mr. Bryan on this subject.

But it is said that the attitude of the Republican candidate for the Presidency is hostile to labor. I deny this. There is no man in public life who has greater sympathy with the lawful purposes of labor in organizing for its own protection and in seeking to maintain the rate of wages and other favorable terms of employment than I have. It is true that in a number of cases I have had to decide against labor, just as in a number of cases I have had to decide against combinations of capital. The questions turn on the particular set of circumstances and evidence and the law as applied to them, and if as a judge I had manifested any bias one way or the other, I should not now be entitled to the support of the people at large for the Presidency; but I am sure it will be found, upon examination of my opinions, that I laid down the law with impartiality, without fear or favor, and without regard to the question whether plaintiffs or defendants were corporations, laboring men, business men, or professional men.

It is now charged by Mr. Bryan that my desire to oppress labor is shown because in one instance during the very hard times of 1894–95 I declined to modify an order of the receiver appointed by my court reducing the wages of employees of a railway company 10 percent. That is true. But it was because the order had only been made in the extremity presented by the deplorable business conditions of that time, and the peculiar circumstances under which the road was being operated. The roadbed was owned by the city of Cincinnati, which had leased the road to the Cincinnati, New Orleans and Texas Pacific Railway Company at a rental of $83,000 a month. The railway company had no property except leasehold, and it was necessary, in order that any property should be left at all, lest a complete forfeiture take place, that the rent should be paid under the leasehold. The payment of the rent was the only means by which the property of the company could be preserved. The net receipts in the previous two months had fallen as low as $43,000 a month, leaving a constantly growing deficit, which the receiver was unable to meet by borrowing more money. He had exhausted all credit. All sorts of economies had been resorted to until the point of actual safety in the operation of the road was reached, and it became necessary, therefore, as a last resort to reduce the wages of the men 10 percent. Such a reduction had been put in force a considerable period before, by all other railroads centering in Cincinnati and this reduction was adopted by the receiver as a last resort. It was impossible for the receiver to borrow money because he had only the leasehold to pledge as security and no capitalist would lend more money upon that. Under these circumstances, most reluctantly the court was obliged to refuse to modify the order of the receiver reducing the wages. As this was a time when substantially all other railroads in the country had made a similar reduction, it was impossible to avoid it and save the property. It is said that the men were not given a hearing. This is entirely untrue. They were given a full hearing with evidence and argument in their behalf by able counsel and this though precedents did not justify that course.

It is pointed out that Judge Caldwell in another case refused to permit such a reduction, but in the case of Judge Caldwell, he had in his court jurisdiction over the whole body of the road upon which money could be borrowed by receiver's certificates with a priority of lien, in order to continue its operation, whereas no such condition existed in the case in which I made the ruling. It was a case upon which I passed judicially. I called in another judge to assist me. The evidence taken was extensive, and the argument by counsel on both sides was at great length, and the result reached was the only one consistent with the continued operation of the road.

I am not apologizing for the action but only explaining it, and pointing out that no other course could have been taken by me conscientiously as a judge. It was not followed by a strike, for the men acquiesced in the result, recognizing it as one of absolute necessity.

In the matter of wages, it has come to me officially to determine the question of the proper wages of employees when I was acting in an executive capacity at the head of the Panama Canal construction, and it will be found that I have generally approved the fixing of wages satisfactory to the men employed on that great work, with proper allowances for the difference between the conditions existing on the Isthmus and those surrounding similar employment at home, and that I have always opposed a limitation upon the discretion of the War Department in the matter of fixing wages, and that this fact has been recognized gratefully by the Steam Shovelers' Union in a resolution making me an honorary member of that body. I approved the advance of the wages of locomotive engineers, of locomotive firemen, of steam shovelmen and of cranemen.

The second case was Moores and Company against the Bricklayers' Union. Moores and Company were lime dealers. The Bricklayers' Union had a fight and a strike with a boss bricklayer. It notified every material man in Cincinnati that it would boycott any material man who sold materials to the boss bricklayer. Moores and Company unconsciously did so, and a walking delegate found it out. A boycott was declared against Moores and Company. Their business was destroyed—a valuable one. They brought suit before a jury, and I was the judge that charged the jury, and I told them that that was a secondary boycott; that it was an attempt to involve a third person in an industrial controversy by duress, in respect to which he had no normal relation, and that any injury that grew out of that the person injured might recover for in a suit for damages against the person instituting the boycott. That was the law then; it is the law now; it is so decided by every Supreme Court in the United States and the Supreme Court of the United States, and it ought to be the law. Not only that, but the best labor unions today recognize that the use of a secondary boycott in industrial disputes is very bad policy. It is the use of an un-American and un-Republican instrument of tryanny, and it ought to be stamped out, Mr. Samuel Gompers to the contrary notwithstanding. He is asking Congress, and has been for the last five years, to pass an act legalizing boycotts, and until Mr. Bryan answers Mr. Roosevelt's questions, we must assume that he also favors the legality of secondary boycotts.

Now the third case was this: Mr. P. M. Arthur was the chief of the Brotherhood of Locomotive Engineers. He was one of the greatest labor leaders they ever had in this country, and his brotherhood has always been one of the most useful and one of the most intelligently conducted and one of the most successful. But they made one mistake. They had what they called "Secret Rule No. 12," and under that rule the engineers on a connecting line were directed not to haul the cars of a line with which the Brotherhood had a strike.

The Toledo & Ann Arbor road had a strike with the brotherhood. I heard that the Lake Shore was going to refuse to haul the cars of that line because of the difference with their engineers. It filed a bill for an injunction to compel the Lake Shore, its officers and employees, to haul the cars. The injunction was issued by Judge Ricks. Subsequently Mr. Arthur issued a telegram to the engineers of the Lake Shore, calling their attention to Rule No. 12, and in effect directing them as engineers to refuse to haul the cars.

The statute of the United States provides, in the Interstate Commerce Law, that any railway corporation, any officer or any employee of a railway corporation refusing to haul the cars of a connecting line shall be subject to fine and imprisonment. I was notified in a proper form by petition that Mr. Arthur had issued that telegram to his engineers on the Lake Shore road, and I issued an order to him requiring him to recall that telegram. He did recall the telegram. He was a law-abiding man. And the case was then heard at length and the order sustained. It never has been reversed to this day. There was a right of appeal if anybody had desired to take it.

I have been criticised for language used in the opinion concerning the Rule No. 12, the enforcement of which was a violation of the statute of the United States already referred to. The language which I used was this:

"We have thus considered with some care the criminal character of Rule No. 12 and its enforcement, not only because, as will presently be seen, it assists in determining the civil liabilities which grow out of them, but also because we wish to make plain, if we can, to the intelligent and generally law-abiding men who compose the Brotherhood of Locomotive Engineers, as well as to their usually conservative chief officer, what we cannot believe they appreciate, that, notwithstanding their perfect organization, and their charitable, temperance, and other elevating and most useful purposes, the existence and enforcement of Rule No. 12, under their organic law, make the whole brotherhood a criminal conspiracy against the laws of their country."

The effect of this statement was to induce the Brotherhood, as was hoped, to abolish Rule No. 12. I was nevertheless held up to execration as a judge who had violated all the laws, and had oppressed trades unionism and made it impossible to exist. It was represented that I had enjoined a man to continue in the service, and had prevented him from striking. Now, as a matter of fact, I wrote a very carefully prepared opinion—I suppose it was too long; it must have been or Mr. Bryan would have read it. It must have been or else the chiefs of the orders would have read it. The truth is, if it had not been so long I would not be here engaged in the somewhat unusual business of expounding my own decisions. But in that case I laid down these principles which I think had never been collated and stated in this way before, athough they were the existing law.

The first was this: That any employee may absolutely leave the employment of his employer without question, whether he breaks a contract or not and no injunction will lie to prevent; that he may associate with his fellow-employees and bring about what is called a strike, and no injunction will issue to prevent that; that he may organize his fellow-employees into associations, who shall appoint officers, and they may refer these industrial disputes to their officers to abide by their decision, and may give to the officers the power of exclusion from the association for disobedience; that they may by assessment collect a fund to support strikers, if strikes are thought necessary; that they may withdraw from association with their employers, and withdraw those who sympathize with them from such association; but that they may not injure the property or unlawfully injure the business of their employers, and they may not institute a secondary boycott in such a dispute.

Now I was not running for office. I had a life position, and I could afford to wait to be vindicated. About six or eight years afterward these same orders got into difficulty with the Missouri Pacific road. The conductors, engineers and trainmen all thought that they were not paid enough by Mr. Gould. Accordingly the chiefs met in St. Louis, and after conducting negotiations, were unable to reach a conclusion and ordered a strike. The railroad company employed a lawyer, who went into court with a bill in equity to enjoin those chiefs from intermeddling between the railway company and their employees, on the ground that they were persuading them to break contracts and to do all sorts of things. That injunction was issued, and then these chiefs followed a course which it might be well for a good many labor organizations to follow—they employed a good lawyer, not a lawyer who thought it his business to abuse the courts, but a lawyer who knew the law and who tried to help the courts in reaching a just and legal conclusion. They consulted him and he said: "This injunction is too broad. I can get it modified." They said: "We are glad of it." "Yes," he said, "I have a case, the authority of which settles it." They said: "What case is that?" He said: "It is the case of P. M. Arthur, the one decided by Judge Taft." Well, one of the chiefs who was there told me this about a month ago. They said: "Is there anything in that case that helps us in any other?" "Yes," he said, "it lays down the principles upon which your association is conducted, if it is conducted legally." So, as he said to me: "We thought your decision was pretty stiff but I did not read it at the time—I did not read it until we found that it helped us, and then when I did read it I found that you had laid down the law which is the Magna Charta upon which all trade organizations of this country stand."

Now Mr. Gompers says that I have said that he has misrepresented me. I have said so. He has misrepresented me as being hostile to labor and an enemy of labor. What I say is that trades unionism has flourished, has become useful to its members, and to society, and has become powerful under the rules of law that I laid down more than a decade ago, and that instead of being denounced as hostile and unfair to labor, I am entitled, in so far as a judge is entitled who lays down the law as he believes it, to be regarded as the benefactor of trades unionism and labor.

There was another case, the Phelan case, which grew out of the Debs insurrection. Mr. Eugene V. Debs, with whom I am running for the Presidency, was at the head of the American Railway Union, and he conceived the idea that it was a proper thing to regulate the wages paid by Mr. Pullman to his employees by tying up every railroad in the country, starving the babies and families until the country should take Mr. Pullman by the neck, so to speak, and compel him to pay the wages to his employees that Mr. Debs thought he ought to pay them. That was a secondary boycott on an enormous scale, and Mr. Debs carried it further than anybody thought it was possible when he began. He sent Mr. Phelan down to Cincinnati. Mr. Phelan learned that one railroad there was in the hands of a receiver whom I had appointed. He called the employees of the receiver together, and he sought to persuade them to go out. Most of them would not go out. He called in men of other railroads and he told them to persuade those men of the receiver to go out and, if they would not be persuaded, to kick them out. They were members of the old orders, and as they would not go out the result was that their heads were broken by brickbats thrown at them. They were also assaulted on their way home to Ludlow, Kentucky, and nearly beaten to death. I had to station constables and marshals upon those engines, and when this condition was brought to my attention properly, I sent for Mr. Phelan with a warrant of arrest, and I brought him into court and enjoined him from continuing that conduct, which continued for not less than two weeks during which I was trying him. At the end of two weeks I convicted him on overwhelming evidence, and I sent him to jail for six months as he richly deserved. I did not send him to jail for the crimes or offense against the law that he had committed. Those were matters for consideration by the grand jury. I sent him to jail for his flagrant violation of the authority of the court. Being under injunction to discontinue that unlawful conduct, he nevertheless held up to contempt the authority of the court for the Southern District of Ohio. Now I am not here to apologize for anything that I have done in that connection. The authority of the courts must be upheld. If they are not, we might as well go out of the governing business. Combinations of capital are to be encouraged so long as they keep within the law, and combinations of workmen are to be encouraged so long as they keep within the law. When you permit them to exist, you permit in your community a tremendous power to be exercised necessarily by a few men, and you have got to make your courts powerful in order to keep them both within the law.

In order to show that I have no bias against employees of railroads, I may cite two cases in which I decided with them, and which subsequently became noteworthy as having been sustained rather by statutory action than by subsequent judicial action. A railway employee sued for damages for the loss of a leg where his foot was caught in an unblocked frog. The statute of Ohio required the railroad to block the frog and to be subject to a penalty for not doing so. The railroad company set up as a defense that the plaintiff knew that the frog was not blocked and that the employee assumed the risk as soon as he knew it. We held that this principle of assumption of risk actually defeated the purposes of the statute which was to save the lives of the men, and that there was no assumption of risk, and that such an assumption of risk would not constitute a defense. This principle, although contrary to the general weight of authority in the United States has since been adopted by Congress in its statutes affecting relations between interstate railways and employees.

Again, a railway express messenger signed a contract exempting a railway company from liability for damages incurred by the negligence of the railway company. I held that the contract was void and contrary to public policy and this decision was taken to the Supreme Court and reversed by that court, but I am glad to say that Congress, in its Employers' Liability Act, has made a special provision that such a contract shall be regarded as void. I cite these instances to show that there was not the slightest bias on my part toward employees. On the contrary, I was anxious that justice should be done, and that the disadvantage under which they labored in dealing with their employers should be recognized in law, and should be regarded as a reason for avoiding strict construction against them.

I have not always been on the Bench, and my relations have not been confined to judicial decisions. When I was Governor of the Philippines, I took occasion to encourage, as far as possible, the organization of labor unions on proper principles, and to bring about a condition of law there equivalent to that which now exists in America. The head of the American Federation of Labor sent a Mr. Rosenberg, the head of the Miners' Union, to investigate, and he made a report favorable to the attitude of the Civil Governor of the Islands toward trades unionism.

Again, while I was in charge of the Panama Canal and its construction for four years, I had much to do with labor, and, as already said, I had to fix wages and agree upon the terms of employment when an appeal was taken to me by the men. The report of the Labor Investigating Commission and the action of the Steam Shovelers' Union in making me a member of their organization, already referred to, would seem to indicate that I had not been unfair to labor there.

And now Mr. Fuller, representing the railway trainmen, comes forward and charges me with attempting to abrogate the Eight Hour Law. What I did was to recommend that the Eight Hour Law be not applied to alien workmen. The reasons for the Eight Hour Law in the United States have no application whatever to the working of the West Indian negroes, and the foreign labor in the Torrid Zone, and can have no effect upon the principle underlying that act. This was the view of President Roosevelt, emphatically expressed to Mr. Gompers, and was the view taken by the Republican party, and I am quite content to abide by that position.

I was Secretary of War for four years, and the War Department probably employs more labor under contract than any other department, or private corporation, and this brought me into contact especially with workmen engaged in dredging, and in river and harbor work. I have had conferences with respect to the Eight Hour Law and in respect to other matters with the heads of unions, and have always reached a satisfactory conclusion, so much so that Mr. Daniel Keefe, who is a member of the Executive Council of the American Federation of Labor, an associate of Mr. Gompers, has thought it consistent with his duty to announce his support of me for the Presidency and to certify that he always found me fair to labor.

Were this a contest in which my individual interests were alone concerned, I should hesitate to discuss my opinions and judicial acts and executive acts, and should prefer to let them stand or fall by the written explanation given in the opinion or in the executive decision, but as there is a disposition on the part of my opponents to decline to read anything on the subject, and as I should feel very much disappointed to have acts of mine misconstrued and injure the cause of Republicanism, I have thought it necessary to go into a full explanation of all the acts of mine which were made the basis of criticism. I am not apologizing for any of the decisions rendered or any of the executive acts performed. I am merely stating them and avoiding the misconstruction and false charges in regard to them made by partisans in this campaign.

Mr. Gompers' announcement as to his agreement with the Democratic party and Mr. Bryan is that they propose to interject a jury trial between an order of the court and its enforcement for all contempts committed outside the presence of the court, and the argument is that if a convicted thief, if charged a second time, must be tried by a jury, why should not a man who violates the order of the court? The reason is that it is of the highest importance to preserve the power of the court to enforce its own orders. Now, why do they make a distinction between indirect contempts and direct contempts—that is, why do they distinguish between contempts committed in the presence of the court and those committed outside? The reason for the exception that they will give at once will be that it is in order to preserve the authority of the courts. Is there any more reason why a man who raises a row in court and is sentenced to jail for thirty days should not have a trial, than a man who violates an order of the court? In each case the reason why he should not have a jury trial is the same. It is to preserve the authority of the court, and the very fact that they have an opportunity to send a man to jail without a jury trial for contempts committed in the presence of the courts gives the whole case away. It shows that there is a reason why we should not have a jury trial in some cases where those cases are necessary to sustain the authority of the court.

Now, let me explain to you the operation of the proposed change. An indirect contempt is the violation of a subpœna by a witness. One of your Federal judges here issues a subpœna to John Smith, and John Smith for some reason or other does not want to come to court to testify. So he does not come that day, and the next day he is sent for. The marshal is sent for him and he is brought into court. The judge says: "The marshal says he served the subpœna on you personally. Why were you not here?" "Excuse me, Judge, I am familiar with the recently enacted Democratic statute, and I decline to answer. You will have to summon twelve men in a box here to determine first whether your marshal tells the truth—I decline to answer. Perhaps your marshal tells the truth, perhaps he does not, but these twelve men have got to settle it before you can act on it."

Suppose you issue a summons to a juror. The juror wants to go fishing, and he relies on this Democratic statute. He is finally brought in in a day or two, and he is asked if he did not get the juror summons. He says: "Excuse me, Judge. I am familiar with the statutes. You will have to summon another jury to determine whether I was properly summoned as a juryman." That shows the utter absurdity of the law. It shows how far men will go in weakening fatally the power of the courts in order to achieve some partisan purpose. But that is not all. The worst of it is in the adjudicated orders of the court that have been fully considered. Take this case. An inventor of note, like most inventors, with very little money, after working hard, gets a patent. A wealthy corporation tries to buy it from him and they cannot agree on terms. So they consult an astute patent lawyer, and he tells them he hopes he can get them out of it and they go ahead and infringe the patent. The inventor scrapes together $5,000 or $10,000 and he fights that case, as they have to fight it in such a case two or three years. Finally he gets a decree affirming the validity of his patent and its value as an invention, and the fact that the defendant infringes it. Then the defendant corporation takes the case up, and the inventor is kept dancing in the courthouse another year, and it costs him $3,000 or $4,000 more. Then there is a decree affirming the decree of the court below, and then by some hook or crook they move for a certiori in the Supreme Court of the United States, and they carry it up there, and it costs him $2,500 more; but finally he gets a decree in the Supreme Court of the United States, and a mandate that is sent down to the court below to enforce that judgment. The counsel for the infringing company have studied this Democratic statute, and they advise their clients that there is still a way out, and that they may go ahead with their infringement. So they go ahead with their infringement, and then this inventor who has labored and borrowed all the money he could, and starved himself during these four or five years, comes into court and asks the Judge to punish them for attempting to violate an order which has passed through three courts and been confirmed. The Judge says: "I would be glad to, for this is a flagrant case, but the Democratic statute, with which you are familiar, requires me now on your charge to secure a jury to determine whether this company is actually infringing your patent which has been declared to be valid and which three courts have declared that that company is infringing, but you still have got to subject that nice, delicate question to the uncertainties of twelve laymen that are to sit in the box and pass on the case."

I submit to any honest-minded man, whether to put in a provision of that sort thus holding up to ridicule and weakening the solemn orders of three courts, reached with all the deliberation possible, is not laying the axe at the foot of the tree of justice and destroying the authority of the courts. I do not care what its effect is on my political future. As long as I have the strength to do so, I shall protest against any weakening of the power of the courts, and especially in this day of human progress when we have to depend more on the courts and their power and the purity of justice and its strength than ever before in the history of the world. There is not an issue in this campaign comparable in importance to the attack on the courts—the insidious attack on the courts that is being made by Mr. Samuel Gompers and his partner, Mr. William Jennings Bryan.

Before the wage-earner finally makes up his mind as to the party which he should support, he ought in the interest of himself and his family to consider the more general reasons why the Democratic party and its policies should be defeated in this election. This is because the election of a Democrat and a Democratic Congress would mean business disaster to the country. The introduction of the tariff for revenue system in substition of the tariff for protection would inevitably involve us in a similar business disaster as that which we had in '93, '94, '95 and '96, whereas the election of the Republican ticket will insure a thorough, genuine revision of the tariff on the protective principle, and will not destroy our industries.

We have had a panic, followed by an industrial depression, from which we are just recovering. Mr. Bryan says that it is a Republican panic that it occurred during a Republican administration. That is true, but it followed a period of immense prosperity, and was brought about by undue confidence in the business situation which led to over-investment and the engaging of liquid capital in many enterprises that proved not to be lucrative or profitable. The liquid capital of the world was largely absorbed by the losses of war and by this over-investment. The revelations concerning corporate mismanagement, corporate lawlessness in this country, and infidelity of financial trust obligations on the part of some prominent men, created a lack of confidence especially in Europe, the liquid capital was absorbed and hoarded, railroads were unable to borrow money. Finally the crash came, and a depression has followed which has been felt in business and manufacturing circles. The panic is not a general panic, but only one dependent on its existence for the peculiar conditions I have mentioned. It will not settle down into a general panic unless the result of the next election destroys the confidence which is gradually returning, and with it the prosperity of two years ago. The election of Mr. Bryan will destroy this confidence, and be a menace to prosperity. It could not be otherwise in view of his record, the instability of his economic views, his persistent recommendation of the policy of repudiation involved in the free coinage of silver for three successive campaigns, his favoring the government ownership of railroads as the only means by which the railroads can be properly regulated and controlled, his guarantee of bank deposits, which involves the socialistic taxation of a good banker to pay the debts of a poor, dishonest or negligent banker. All such nostrums and panaceas, which will never work a cure, have made all conservative persons in the country distrust Mr. Bryan and the accuracy and safety of his economic views. Hence his election will destroy confidence and will continue the present depression. Every person interested in a restoration of prosperity should vote against him.

16

A Few Words to Southern Democrats

Delivered at Augusta, Georgia, January 14, 1909, in Reply to a Speech of Welcome to the South and an Invitation to Visit South Carolina and the City of Anderson

Mr. Mayor and Citizens of Anderson:

The first proposition I am going to make to you is to put on your hats. I do not want to be responsible for any pneumonia; I do not want to be limited in my remarks by the feeling that possibly their extension might cause such a misfortune.

I am very grateful to you for this substantial evidence of your welcome of me to the South. The presence here of so many successful and prominent citizens of a town like Anderson, which I believe has sometimes been called the Lowell of the South, where time means money, where time is important to you all, I should like to have you know I deeply appreciate. Coming so far and in such numbers and under these circumstances, I value much the expression of your hospitable welcome. Your description of Anderson squares with the description which I presume may be given to quite a number of towns, not all of them perhaps so fortunately situated throughout the South, in which there is today that spirit of civic pride, that determination to make the towns go forward that characterizes, and has for the last ten years, characterized, the civilization and the people of the South. They have come to share the prosperity of the Nation in such a way that they have enjoyed rather more of the prosperity than those of us in the North, and I am glad that it is so.

Under conditions which, for a time, seemed to make permanent the disastrous effects of the War, it was impossible to have the traces of that division between us wiped out entirely. But when we are all prosperous, when we are all making money, when we are all able to educate our children and to give our wives and our families comfortable homes, and when we think that we are successful and are accomplishing everything in the world and are doing things, we become philosophical, we become willing to let bygones be bygones, and to forget everything of the past that we ought to forget, and to remember only the brotherhood that exists and ought to exist between all the citizens under the starry flag.

Now, you have said you were Democrats. Well, I suppose you are, most of you, Democrats; but I haven't got anything against you on that ground. We must have parties in this country. It is not possible to have eighty millions of people, with sixteen million voters, carry on a government unless we do have parties which shall form a machine, so to speak, for reducing the varying views of sixteen million of the electorate, or a majority of that electorate, to a resultant force which shall effect and carry out the public will. We have got to subordinate a good many of our views in order to make a common view which shall be manifest in the carrying on of the Government. We wish to avoid as far as we can that division into little groups which is seen in many of the European countries where they attempt constitutional government, and which results in a lack of a consistent policy because there is no majority responsible to carry on the Government. We have avoided that thus far in this country, and I hope that we may.

All that we can hope for, all that we ought to ask is that the people of all sections shall make up their minds in an independent way, and then vote for the principles that they favor. The result is all that any patriotic citizen can ask. Whether it brings about the success of one party or of another, we can generally count on the intelligence, the patriotism, and the foresight of the majority of the American people, whichever party tag they bear, as a party to carry on a good government, a government in which we shall uphold the institutions left to us by our fathers, maintaining freedom and liberty and the institutions of private property, and those other guaranties contained in our Constitution.

We, in a sense, are the most conservative people in the world. That is because we know a good thing when we see it, and we propose to keep it. There may be changes and amendments necessary in the law to effect reforms that have impressed their necessity on us during the last ten years. Doubtless there are. But I think, certainly in the South and generally through the country, we do not wish to destroy that government or so change it as to make it different from that which our fathers and forefathers contemplated in the formation and maintenance of the Constitution, entered upon in 1789.

I know that sometimes the Constitution seems to be in the way of direct effectiveness. The division under our system by which the central government is limited to certain things and the state governments carry on other things, sometimes seems to work against the rapid carrying out of some of the reforms, as for instance, the conservation of our natural resources, and, perhaps, the regulation of railroads and the suppression of those abuses which have crept in with our marvelous progress in the combinations of capital. And yet, gentlemen, that Constitution, simple, clear and comprehensive, has in the past been capable of such fair construction as to meet in a marvelous way the developments and emergencies of our country which could not have been anticipated by those who framed it, and I am very certain that the same Constitution will meet the emergencies which may come in the future.

What we look to in the South is to have the support of those institutions from the people who believe in them and are willing to maintain them, and to fight for them, if it be necessary.

Now, my friends, I cannot fail to express to you the feeling that bubbles up in me, of gratitude for the very cordial reception that I have had since I came south of Mason and Dixon's line; and at no meeting have I found it more emphatic than at this one; in no reception have the circumstances made it any more impressive than in this one, which you have been good enough to tender me, of the citizens of Anderson, South Carolina.

I congratulate Anderson on her prosperity. I have no doubt that when I come again into the South the statistics will be added to. I have no doubt if I were to institute a search into the pockets of the gentlemen here, I should find, as I have found in some other parts of the country, papers containing statistics on the subject of the growth of Anderson.

I am glad that this is so. I am glad that it is written in the heart and mind of every citizen that he feels pride in the town in which he lives. I sincerely hope that that pride manifests itself, as doubtless it does, in the maintenance of a good government there, in control of men who are honest, who believe in civic righteousness, and who are giving you a city in which you are proud to live and of which you are proud to be citizens.

17

The Winning of the South

Delivered at Atlanta, Georgia, January 15, 1909

Mr. Chairman, Gentlemen of Atlanta, and Atlanta's Guests:

I came South to Augusta to obtain rest from a nervous strain due to a campaign of public speaking. This was the avowed and the real purpose of my visit to Summerville, that suburb of Augusta upon the sand hills, whence it is possible to look over into the promised land of the dispensary. Before I left Washington and in the hurry of that capital, I was honored by a visit from a committee of eloquent, mellifluous and sweet-spoken gentlemen headed by your distinguished, handsome and impressive Governor, who secured from me a promise to visit that city which they said was more fully representative of the energy, enterprise, business courage and modesty of the South than any other. No sooner had I accepted the invitation than I began to realize that Atlanta was the place of all others for a man in search of rest to avoid. Rising from its own ashes some forty years ago, this city and its inhabitants have led the strenuous life in the marvelous growth and development of the city, and no man could expect a rest so long as he was in its custody and under its control. Only three cities suggest the spirit of

non-partisan character of the welcome which has been so kindly extended to me.

Now, if this indirectly makes, not for a partisan advantage, but for a continuance of the movement in favor of independence of speech and action and political tolerance its result is one that all citizens of whatever political party must rejoice to have brought about. The relation of the National Administration to a section like this, in the distant past, has been that almost of an alien government or at least of a government like that of a home government to a colony. The direct local effect of a national administration upon the South is chiefly through its local officials, appointed and exercising their functions through the section, and therefore the expression of the Administration toward the Southern people takes its colour in the character of those officials, and, therefore, the Administration may be properly held accountable and its policy determined by the qualifications, fitness and standing of the men appointed to represent it in the districts and states of the section. I realize, therefore, that expressions of sympathy with the South and an earnest desire to bring it closer to the central government in thought and action and feeling will have comparatively little weight unless this expression is accompanied by such appointments in the South as shall prove this sympathy to be real and substantial. The difficulty of making proper selections in a part of the country where the sensibilities of the people are different from those of one's own section, where conditions of society differ so radically, and where there are no accredited representatives selected by the people of the same party as the Administration, is very great indeed. It is a question of evidence and of evidence difficult to get, and when secured, hard to weigh, because it is only judgment and estimate and generally not a mere statement of a concrete fact. All I can say with reference to the future policy of the Administration in the South on this subject is that I expect to spare no effort to find out the facts in respect to the character of the proposed appointees, and so far as in me lies to select those whose character and reputation and standing in the community commend them to their fellow-citizens as persons qualified and able to discharge their duties well, and whose presence in important positions will remove, if any such thing exists, the sense of alienism in the Government which they represent.

The work of the next Administration is to be a work of creation and construction, to furnish the machinery with which the great principles announced and carried forward to successful establishment by Theodore Roosevelt are to be clinched and maintained. The legislation affecting the great railway and industrial corporations needs amendment, not so much to change its principle or object, as to facilitate its enforcement and make its violation less easy and advisable.

Of course, the immediate great work of the Administration must be the revision of the tariff. In that work the South is quite as much interested as the North, and would have an honest genuine revision such as has been promised by the party in power.

The continuance of our Philippine policy, with the improvement in the commercial relations between the Islands and the United States we may reasonably anticipate, and in that commercial improvement there is no section of the country more interested than the South.

The great field of diplomatic care, attention and activity for the next thirty or forty years, so far as this country is concerned, is likely to be in the far Orient. The oriental trade which involves so much sale of metal products and of cotton products most nearly concerns the welfare of the South. All these policies, therefore, may well call for the close scrutiny of those who are leaders of industry in Atlanta and other cities and ought to awaken on their part a desire to exercise the legitimate influence that such a section as this ought to exercise in respect to the phases of the policies to be pursued. All I can do is to assure the Southern people that no interest of the South, whether it share that interest with the North, or whether it has a peculiar interest of its own, will be neglected in the conduct of the Government, in so far as that conduct shall be under the control of its Chief Executive.

I am glad that I came to Atlanta. I am glad to meet this most cordial, and graceful hospitality and welcome extended to me as the coming President. I beg those of my hearers who differ from me politically not to suppose that their cordial and courteous reception are misunderstood by me. I know that they spring from an earnest and patriotic desire to pay proper respect to the great office to which I have been elected, and that they grow out of a sincere wish and proper assumption that, having been elected to the Chief Magistracy, I shall become the President not of a party but of a whole united people.

18

Hopeful Views of Negro Difficulties

Delivered in Big Bethel Church, Atlanta, Georgia, January 16, 1909

Bishop Gaines, Professor Matthews, Ladies and Gentlemen:

I am very glad to be here in this presence. Had circumstances prevented me from having an opportunity of meeting my colored fellow-citizens in my visit to Georgia, I should have thought it a great misfortune for me. I should have regarded my visit to Georgia as not complete in failing to meet a part of the citizenship of this section in whose development, in whose progress, in whose prosperity I have the profoundest interest, and with whose efforts to uplift themselves I have the deepest sympathy. It is true that in your history and in the consideration of what has happened in the past, and possibly what will happen in the future, it is difficult to exclude political conditions and to avoid discussing your present and your future political issues. But you will understand me, I am sure, when I say to you that here as the coming President, should the Lord permit me to live until the 4th of March, I must stand as the representative of all the people and avoid in every way partisan and political discussion; but I can conceive that the President of the United States can have no more sacred function than to offer words of encouragement, of suggestion, and of hope to those to whom fate in the past has not been kind and with respect to whom the whole American people has the highest obligation of trusteeship and guardianship. Now we know a great deal more today than we knew thirty years ago, all of us, whether on one side or the other. We know that we were not always right in every particular ourselves, and that the other side, who differed from us, was not always wrong in every particular, and we can afford, in the progress that has been made, to rejoice that the progress makes assurance of further progress and further prosperity for all of us. One of the things that the past teaches us, one of the things that it impresses on every man who gives earnest consideration to the working out of the providence of God, is that in the man himself must he find the seeds of his progress. I say to you colored men and colored women of this country that, hard as your lot has been, and hard as the road is likely to be onward and upward, if you will abide by the judgment of your conscience, by those very ideals that lead to self-restraint, to honest effort, to providence, you will attain a condition in the future that you hardly dream of today. Look back to what you were forty years ago. Your people were not, 5 percent of them, able to read or write, and today you have reached nearly the figure of 50 percent of literacy among you, and you must consider the conditions and the hard conditions, under which that improvement has been made. Brought here against your will, put here in a condition of slavery for years and years, and then made the subject of a bloody war, this country, to which your fortunes must always be attached, reduced to a condition of poverty and straitened circumstances so that it was almost impossible for the white owners of property to live, much less those who had no property and no education, yet, under those circumstances, you have gone on so that today a large part of the farming—I could give you the statistics—is in the hands of the colored people of the South and dotted over the South are model places which show to you what can be done when you approach your problems with common sense and a determination to recognize the facts that stand before you, and to meet those facts with courage and bravery. I do not intend to discuss race feeling and race prejudice, because the discussion of it and the argument of it never did anybody good. You must recognize facts, and in the face of those facts, because they cannot keep you down, you can go on to a brighter and brighter future. Every one of you knows in his heart, because every one knows noble, earnest, sympathetic white men in the South, that your greatest aid and your greatest hope is in the sympathy and the help of those white men who are your neighbors; and I thank God that in the South there is developing fast evidence of a stronger and stronger sympathy with the effort to uplift the race among the white men of the South, who feel themselves responsible for the whole Southern civilization. Your people have faults that grow out of your history and your training, but the first step and indication in an improvement of faults is the knowledge that you have them, and when you read in the sermons of your own people, in the lectures of your own people, the cold—I won't call it cold, because it is not cold—but the sympathetic truth in respect to yourselves and the necessities that present themselves to you in your path upward, one of the greatest steps possible has been achieved. You have among you men who do credit to the entire American manhood. No one can read the life of Booker Washington and know what he has done, without being proud that our country has produced such a man, and I say it without invidious distinction, because there are, doubtless, others that deserve similar tribute; but it has come to me personally to know him and to be associated with him, and to understand the marvelous perception that he has into the future of your race and the necessities that are presented to you in winning a higher place in life. Of course, the first thing is education. The first thing is to give every man who is to enjoy civil rights knowledge enough to know what these rights are, and how he can protect himself in them. Of course, it is a great mistake either among white men or colored men, to think that because a man gets a university education, therefore he is better than other people or in a better condition. Whether the university education does him good or not depends upon the foundation of character that he has. You need among you, as the white men need among them, university education for the leaders, your ministers who control so much of your opinion, your physicians, and there ought to be a great many more of them well educated, in order to teach the race the rules of hygiene that in the country are so often widely departed from. And you need in all branches of the profession, because you must have leaders among them, the opportunity for giving them the best education that the world affords, but that is a comparatively small number. The great body of the race are those who are to be the workers, the manual workers, and what is needed for the great body of your race is primary and industrial education, so that you shall commend yourselves to the community in which you live as absolutely indispensable to its proper and future growth and prosperity; that when you have carpenters they shall be honest carpenters who know their craft that your blacksmiths, your machinists and all those who engage in manual labor, skilled or unskilled, shall have the intelligence and the knowledge to make them as good as possible in rendering the service for which they are to receive a just compensation.

Now, my friends, I did not come here prepared to make a speech. And I always come before an audience of your race with a great deal of hesitation because your race is a musical race and it is an oratorical race, and I am neither musical nor oratorical. But I did want to come here because I know the hardships in your road; I know every once in a while that you fall on your knees and pray to God to relieve you from your burdens that you have, and I believe that the expression of sympathy is the one that helps people along; it helps me along, but in that expression of my sympathy I would not have you for a moment abate the thought of the duty imposed on every one of you of making as much of the talent that the Lord gives you as you can.

19

The Young Men's Christian Association

*Delivered under the Auspices of the Colored Y. M. C. A., at the
Tabernacle Baptist Church, Augusta, Georgia, January 17, 1909*

My Fellow-citizens:

I am glad to be here. I should have been better satisfied if I could
have sat for an hour and heard the eloquence of your Dr. Walker, whose
reputation as a minister of the Gospel and as a man who speaks not only
eloquence but sense, has reached into the far North.

I always come before an audience like this with a great deal of hesitation, because you know what eloquence is, and I haven't any to give you.
I know the wide influence for good Dr. Walker exercises in this community. I was glad to hear him speak of the good feeling that exists between
the white and the colored races in this community, and I doubt not that
his words, his leadership and his common sense have greatly contributed
to that end so devoutly to be wished.

This is a Young Men's Christian Association meeting. I find myself
here under circumstances that require an explanation why I am here. Until
I went to the Philippines, I knew of the Young Men's Christian Association
generally, knew something of its work, but had no close association with
it and no personal knowledge of its exellent operation and work. When I

came back from the Philippines, fortunately or unfortunately—perhaps you will think unfortunately before I get through—I was invited by chance to make an address on the Young Men's Christian Association, in Dayton, Ohio. Now, there are lines of wireless telegraphy between all Young Men's Christian Associations in the world, I think, because I never have stopped over Sunday in any place on the globe that I haven't been invited to deliver an address on the Young Men's Christian Association; and so it has fallen to my lot to speak to that Association in Omaha, in Seattle, in Springfield, Massachusetts, in Minneapolis, in Manila, in Shanghai, in Hongkong, and I don't know how many other places.

The object of the Association, as I understand it, is to be an adjunct to all churches, for it knows no difference among them, in filling the leisure time of young men with rational amusement and offering to them the means of spending that time so that they need not yield to the temptations of vice and depart from the path of virtue. That is the object of the Association. It has many others, but that is the principal object; to occupy the leisure of the young man in a city where his steps are beset by temptations to waste his money, if nothing worse—but generally to spend his money in drinking, gambling and other vices that finally lead him to the gutter. You will find that the men who have built up the city are the men who have come to it as boys from the country. They come to the city and their time—much of it—is their own. If they are lawyers, from personal experience I can say their days are largely their own for several years. And so it is with doctors; not of course with ministers, because they don't need the Young Men's Christian Association; but the clerks, the men who are striving to earn a living, have many hours of leisure which, if they can put in in a Christian club where all the influences surrounding them are such as to make them think of better things, and certainly not of worse things, the Young Men's Christian Association is of a value to them which can not be overestimated; it is the best material we have to build up our citizenship, and that thing is as true of the colored people as it is of the white people.

One thing about the Young Men's Christian Association that has always commended itself to me is the very businesslike method that the Association pursues. There is in Springfield a school for the education of Young Men's Christian Association secretaries, and it is about the secretary that every thing in the Association moves. He spends the money as he ought to spend it. He arranges the entertainments; he buys the periodicals; he sees to the various games that are permitted to be played. In other words, he applies to that very necessary thing, the common sense that he has and the experience that has come down to him from years of trial, as to what it is that is most likely to occupy the attention of young men under those circumstances and do them the most good and claim their closest attention. Trained as those secretaries are, you can be very sure that that money goes as far as it can go economically to accomplish the purposes.

It furnishes, therefore, a great opportunity to those men who have more money than they know what to do with, to spend it in such a way as to do good for their fellow-men. It furnishes opportunity for them to put the money where it will do the most good. I don't know how it strikes you. I presume you never had a million dollars to give to somebody else or to do good with; I never had it; but if you could put yourselves in the place of a man who had a million dollars to spend for the good of his fellow-men, I think you would find that it is about as difficult to spend that money so that it will reach the result that you desire and really help your fellow-men, as it was for the man in the first place to make it. Therefore, when we have an opportunity—that is, when you and I become millionaires—and those who now have that opportunity ought to realize it—to spend the money for the benefit of one's fellow-men, the Young Men's Christian Association offers a good place to put as much money in as can be put in the way of doing good to our fellow-men at a time in the lives of our young fellow-men when it is most important.

Then there is another thing about the Young Men's Christian Association that I greatly admire. It recognizes no race, color or creed, but it takes everybody in to assist them. It has introduced into this country more tolerance between religious denominations than any other institution that we have had. Now I want to give you an example of the tolerance that we have reached.

Well, first I think it is a pretty good example that I am elected President of the United States, but I had another thing in my mind, and that is this: when we went to the Philippines we found there a Government that for three hundred years under the Spanish régime had been so united with the Roman Catholic Church that it was very difficult to separate the two. Their interests were so inextricably mixed up that it was most difficult to tell what was the Church's function and what was the civil function of the Government. Now, under the treaty of Paris, all that which really belonged to the Crown of Spain in a civil sense passed to the Government of the United States, but that which belonged to the Roman Catholic Church in that union remained with the Church, and there were presented a great many difficulties of the nicest character, that required all the acumen of the civilian and the canonical lawyers to solve the question where in that separation this particular interest was to fall and that particular interest was to fall. Then in the history of that country the so-called "friars," the monastic orders, had three hundred years before made it a Christian country, for they arrived just about two or three years before the Mohammedans. If they had not, the Islands would have been Mohammedan. As it was, they found Mohammedan tracts there when they went there three hundred years ago, but they found people in such condition that they readily accepted the Christian faith and Christianity spread over those Islands, so that there are now seven million Christians there and they are largely— almost wholly—Christians through the efforts of those monastic orders; and when I say that, I want to emphasize it by pointing out more than that: that the Filipinos are the only people in the Orient who as a people are Christians. Hence the obligation we are all under to those monastic orders for what was done. They went ahead and educated the people in simple arts of agriculture, and they exercised over them a guardianship that kept them as Christians for three hundred years until today. But in the last one hundred years, when the Spaniards came in more freely in the Islands through the Suez Canal, and even before that, when the natives themselves began to have ambitions to become priests, when the question who was to get the best parishes had to be decided, and then when the seeds of Republicanism or a more liberal Government than the Spaniards offered came on, the power that those monks in their parishes exerted was used by the Spanish Government as a sort of police instrumentality for suppressing what they regarded as seditious movements among the people, and that brought about a condition of hatred on the part of the people of these Spanish monastic orders whose predecessors for centuries had been close friends and almost fathers of the people. In the course of those two or three hundred years, the Spanish orders had accumulated by purchase and otherwise, chiefly by purchase, upwards of 400,000 acres of the best lands in the Islands and 250,000 of those acres were distributed in the immediate neighborhood of Manila, in the neighboring provinces where it was easy to carry the products of the lands into the markets in Manila. Those lands were occupied by tenants numbering with their families perhaps 60,000 or more. When Aguinaldo carried on a Government for a month or two in the Islands, they called a so-called constitutional convention, and one of the things they did was to nationalize these lands. That sounds well, but what it means is that they confiscated them and appropriated them to the so-called Filipino Government without paying anything for them. They were the lands the title to which was the least disputed in the Islands. When we went in there and took possession and organized a government and finally brought about tranquillity, and established courts with partly native and partly American judges, these monastic orders under the pledge and covenant of the Treaty of Paris, if for no other reason, were able to go into our courts and say, "Here, we own these lands; for six years we have had no rental for them, and we ask that these tenants be made to pay for this rent or get out." We had the courts there. If courts were to be courts they were entitled to their rights, and yet it meant 60,000 eviction suits. I do not need to tell you, my friends, what that meant. These lands were situated in the Tagalog provinces generally, where most of the sedition had crept in in Spanish times, and where the resistance to our Government between 1900 and 1902 was most bitter, and it meant for us, if we allowed this thing to go on, to have these courts issue the orders of eviction which must be issued under the titles that they had; it meant another revolution. It meant another insurrection. It meant that we should lose of our soldiers thousands of lives and expend millions and millions of dollars in suppressing another insurrection. Something had to be done. They recognized the title of the Filipino Republic under this nationalization, as they called it. They would not pay to the friars but they were logically driven to a recognition of the governmental ownership of the land, so the question was, therefore, whether if we bought the land for our Government and then made easy terms with them we could not bring about a peaceful result. Now, in order to do that, we could not deal with anybody in the Islands. The friars and the heads of the friars were very much prejudiced on the subject, and then they said they did not have the authority—that the authority was with the Pope at Rome. The question was, "What were we to do?" The ordinary, plain method, the American way of doing things, would be to go to the head of the Church. But the trouble was that he was the head of the Roman Catholic Church and it was contrary to our traditions to recognize him as a world power, and all the other denominations might naturally object to introducing diplomatic relations between the United States and the Roman Catholic Church at Rome. So what was done?

Mr. Roosevelt and Mr. Root sent for all the leading preachers of all denominations, and they submitted, not in one conference, but from time to time, these questions to those ministers, and said, "Now, what would you do? We do not want to defeat our administration by doing something that shall shock the sense of the Protestant denominations of this country, but we believe that if the thing is explained to them they will understand that this is the only thing to do and that it does not involve diplomatic relations with a church, but that it is only a plain common sense settlement of an ordinary real estate transaction with such accompaniments as the peculiar circumstances require." The result of those conferences was that those ministers said, "Go ahead, we will stand by you; that is the plain, business way to do things"; and we went ahead.

I went to Rome representing the Government and had conferences with the Pope, with the Cardinals having the authority to deal with this subject, and then they sent an Apostolic delegate to the Islands and for more than a year, we were conducting negotiations and finally we bought those lands for $7,000,000, paid for in the bonds of the Philippine Government, and we held off the law suits until that was done, and we avoided a revolution and all the disasters which would have followed a series of 60,000 evictions. What I say is this, that forty years ago in this country that would have been impossible; that there would have arisen among the denominations an objection to it on the ground that it was a recognition of the Roman Catholic Church, which was contrary to our traditions. But today, under the growing influence of toleration, it was smoothly carried through, and we took a long step toward permanent tranquillity in the Philippines.

I only instance that to say how something has been at work to bring about tolerance between the denominations, to promote the fatherhood of God and the common brotherhood of man, and I believe that the Young

Men's Christian Association has been as strong an influence in that direction as any that I know.

It is perhaps wise to refer to the material and business advantage that arises from the Young Men's Christian Association, and it is a lesson that I think we ought to keep before us. Every well regulated railroad in this country has a Young Men's Christian Association connected with it. Now do you think that that arises because of the overflowing Christian spirit of that corporation? I do not mean to deny to the various directors a charitable disposition. Doubtless each one of them has it, but when they meet together in a board of directors, with an anxiety for dividends, and with a sense of responsibility to their stockholders, that charity disappears. It is a little bit like that story that doubtless you have heard, of the man who wanted to borrow some money at the bank. He went in and saw the president, and the president said, "Well, I might let you have it." Then he saw the cashier, and the cashier hesitated a little bit. He finally said, "Well, I think you might have it, but I would like to speak to the directors." Then the proposed borrower went and saw each director, and each director thought he might have it. Then he went back to the bank and he was presented with a resolution from the whole directorate refusing application for a loan. He turned to them and said, "I have no criticism to make; I believe each one of you is a truthful man, but united you are the worst set of liars I have ever met."

A railroad corporation, therefore, is not going to spend its money in establishing a Young Men's Christian Association if it does not inure to the benefit of the railroad; and it does, it inures in a business way, because it offers to the railway employee a means of spending his leisure time in elevating, moral amusements, in recreation, in study, and it makes him a better railway employee, and enables him to render better and more thorough and more patient and more faithful service to the company.

You could not have a stronger illustration of the benefit of the Young Men's Christian Association from a material and business standpoint than that action of the railroads all over the country.

And so, too, Congress does not appropriate money merely for charitable causes. It is carrying on a great government, and when it runs an army, it does the best it can to make that army efficient. Congress has provided that the Young Men's Christian Association shall be permitted to have today what they call the "post exchange" in every post in the army.

But my attention to the association was called most emphatically in the tropics and in our colonies. Dr. Walker said that some of you had been in Cuba and some of you in the Philippines. If so, you will bear me out in this statement: that you get up in the morning after a good night's rest and you work hard during the day, and you think, "Well, this climate is not any worse than at home; my surroundings are all right and my appetite is good." You seem to be able to do as much work as in a colder country. But after you get through your day's work there comes a time when the vitality seems to lower, when you feel as if you needed some sort of stimulant, and that is the time when the great remedy of the tropics and the Orient is produced in the shape of a bottle, and you are invited to take a little Scotch and soda. Now, you take it and it has the desired effect. The evening is long and there is nothing else to do, and one good turn deserves another, and there is a strong temptation to take a second.

Many a man—I have seen it and I know what I am talking about— who at home would have passed through those moments of temptation without the slightest yielding, there, ten thousand miles away from home, with a sense of distance, and a kind of depression and freedom from the observation and supervision of his neighbors and a sort of lack of responsibility, is led on; and if he yields, as he too frequently does, he embraces all the vices of the Orient, and lands in the gutter either to be a helpless invalid or to die.

There more than at home, more than in any American city, the Young Men's Christian Association offers a means of resisting that temptation. The good effect of it cannot be exaggerated. We have now in Manila, erecting and nearly completed, a Young Men's Christian Association, through the generosity of some one, who contributed, I think, $120,000 if $60,000 or $70,000 was raised among the merchants of Manila. The American merchants are not a large body there, and they have had a pretty poor picking in the way of business too, but they were able to raise that amount and they raised that sum in ten days because they knew that that institution would contribute more directly to the uplifting and the maintenance of the good character of the men whom they had in their employ and possibly even of themselves than any other instrumentality they could have in that community.

So, too, on the Isthmus, where the weather and the circumstances are not unlike those in the Philippines, there is the same temptation, much stronger than it is here. They have the disease which is called "nostalgia," which literally interpreted means "homesickness." It is something more. It is a feeling, "I must get out of this—these beautiful sunsets, these long, warm days, this lazy feeling, this far away from home—I cannot stand it. My nerves are giving away and I must have some means of meeting this." You long for anything. You long for a strap in a street car just to hold yourself up, to make you feel that you are in somebody else's way or that somebody else is in your way. In that kind of desperation you feel so far away from home.

There is nothing like the influence of the Young Men's Christian Association in giving you the means of exercise, tennis courts, billiard tables, bowling alleys, periodicals full of uplifting articles, bathing facilities and everything that goes to make up a decent Christian life under decent Christian auspices. Now on the Isthmus we have established four great clubs, having all these facilities that I have described, and we have paid for them out of the funds for the construction of the canal. We have done it not that we have special authority to do so, but we have done it because we believed we could not take a step more effective in giving us good workmen, in keeping our workmen in a condition where their work would be worth while than by assuring them that during their hours of leisure the time would be passed in such a way as not to interfere with their effectiveness in working the next day.

We pay the salaries of the secretaries that we have drawn from the Young Men's Christian Association in this country, because they are experts in carrying on such institutions and we are going to found two or three more. We pay the ministers on the Isthmus. I think there are some ten or a dozen in our pay, and we keep churches going. It is possible that we will be charged with having filched that money from the public treasury, but if we have, we have accomplished a good work, and I think it can be defended on strictly legal grounds that where you enter a country like the Isthmus of Panama and introduce into it 50,000 souls, some 10,000 or 12,000 whites, some 30,000 or 40,000 colored men and women, unless you take especial pains to have their morality looked after, unless you furnish ministers and churches and Christian clubs, you are going to have such a Saturnalia of vice, such demoralization, that you will never build your canal. Hence, if we are to be impeached for spending that money, it will be in a good cause.

Now, my friends, I have gone over this general discussion of the Young Men's Christian Association and I have come now to its application to this audience, and to the colored people of the South. I am delighted to know that it has taken root here, and I do not know any particular place where that millionaire that you and I spoke of some time ago might put his million any better than in colored Christian associations in the South.

I have the honor to be a member of the Board of Trustees in the distribution of the income of the Jeanes fund for the improvement of rural colored schools in the South, and that is a great work. The schools are not what they ought to be. Doubtless in the cities, I am glad to know from what you say, they are effective, but in the country the terms of instruction, for both white and black, are too short. The salaries paid the teachers are not enough. You have been and so the South has been through a tremendous trial. After the War there was not money enough to furnish schools for anybody. The taxable property was not sufficient. Now you are getting rich in the South, and it seems to me that you are getting more generous in your appropriations for educational purposes, but there is room for great improvement, and anybody that does not want to give money to the Young Men's Christian Association might add to that Jeanes fund. That is another means of distributing wealth in a place where it will do good.

I am deeply sympathetic with the struggle of your race to uplift themselves. I listened with a great deal of interest to what Dr. Walker said with respect to the progress that you have made in Georgia. I had occasion to address the colored people at Bethel Church in Atlanta yesterday, and I ventured to say to them, as I do to you here, that you have your own destiny to carve out. I do not mean to say that you have not obstacles before you, and I deeply sympathize with your feelings with reference to the injustices that arise from prejudice and race feeling, from thoughtless and wicked men. I know how it cuts to the quick, but on the other hand, you know in your hearts, as indeed Dr. Walker has said from this pulpit, that there are in the South many noble white men who believe that the uplifting of the South is largely in the uplifting of the Negro, and he is the chief instrument himself to bring that about.

When you make yourselves indespensable to a community from a material standpoint, there is likely to be a modification of unjust prejudice. The idea that the South can afford to have the Negroes transplanted to some other country always sounded to me like a joke. They tried that down here in Mississippi, and they were only going to move them, not out of the country to Africa, but across the river; and they had a riot. So, of course, that is absurd.

But if the Negro would be respected he must make himself worthy of respect. He must cultivate those virtues of providence, of industry, of thrift, which will make him respected as a laborer, as a farmer, as a skilled mechanic, as a man contributing to the wealth of the community in which he lives and without whose aid the accumulation of that wealth is impossible.

Now, my friends, I have said all I ought to say. I only want to add what I always want to add before a colored audience: that you are Americans. The idea of transplanting you is absurd. The only flag you know is the flag of the Stars and Stripes, and you are of a race which has given up its life and moistened the ground with its blood in defense of that flag, and will continue to do so. Therefore, as the President of the United States to be, if the Lord spares me until the fourth of March, I must feel that I had not discharged my duty in coming into this country if I spoke at all, without speaking to the colored people as an important part of the South, and as Americans entitled to the same earnest concern that I hope the Lord may give me to manifest with respect to a whole united people.

20

The Outlook of Negro Education

Delivered at the Haines Normal and Industrial School,
Augusta, Georgia, January 19, 1909

Bishop Williams, Colonel Lyons, Ladies and Gentlemen:

You have me at a great disadvantage. I have had to talk on the same subject in a good many different places, and a man, if he tells the truth, cannot vary a great deal in what he says. One of the very encouraging and delightful, for I mean, in the strongest sense, signs or facts that I find here is the good mutual feeling between the white and black races in this community. I heard it from the lips of Dr. Walker on Sunday, and I see evidence of it everywhere, and especially in conversation with leading white citizens with whom it has been my pleasure to talk.

Now the thing that impresses me in this meeting is the illustration that it gives of that maxim, which is as true today as it ever was, that "The Lord helps them that help themselves." That a colored woman could have constructed this great institution of learning and brought it to the point of usefulness that it has today, speaks volumes for the capacity of the colored race. You and I don't have to be told or have a history of what she has gone through in the last twenty-five years. We know the hard obstacles she has had to overcome. Of course we know that from time to time, good people lent their aid and gave generously, but the construction of a great institution like this is not done in a day and is not overcome by one act of generosity, but it means a continuous life of hard work, of disinterested unselfishness, of tact, of patience, of willingness to submit at times to humiliating failure, and of confidence in the aid of God in the ultimate result; and, therefore, I shall go out of this meeting, and in spite of the distinguished presence of a great many people here—the Bishop of Georgia, Dr. Walker, the great preacher of your city, Robert C. Ogden, who has done more in the cause of Southern education than any other one man, and others—I shall carry in my memory only the figure of that woman who has been able to create all of this. She must, even in her moments of trial and tribulation, derive immense joy from looking back over the history of her triumph, what she has overcome and what she has accomplished, and when she meets those whom she has sent forth to do the missionary work that they are taught to do, she has the intense satisfaction of receiving in her heart and conscience the verdict to herself of "Well done, thou good and faithful servant."

I do not come into a presence like this without a bursting desire to tell those who hear me of my intense sympathy with a race that is struggling against many obstacles to uplift itself to a higher level, to educate its members and achieve a higher standard of morality and living. I suppose that comes to me more strongly because of the responsibilities that I had in the Philippine Islands for the four years that I was there, and the four years that I subsequently exercised some authority over those Islands, in aiding another race in the far-distant Philippines to lift themselves to a higher standard than that which they had then attained, and to make themselves ultimately worthy of complete self-government. In that expression of sympathy that I wish to give here, I do not feel it inappropriate to refer to some of the expressions that fall from the lips of men prominent in political life that are utterly lacking in any sympathy of that kind, and that are cruel and abrupt in their meaning, if they really are to be given the meaning that the words naturally bear. I refer, for instance, to those gentlemen who deem it necessary to affirm that in the interest of this country the negro race should have no education. I am glad to know and believe that even those men in their hearts do not believe that; that it comes rather from a striking desire to say something that shall have a sensational effect than it does from a real spirit of—I had almost said—cruelty toward a race that deserves from those of us that are white all the aid and all the assistance and all the sympathy that we can possibly give them, considering the circumstances under which they came here. And I know, and you know, that those expressions do not represent the feeling of the great intelligent body of white men in the South.

Now, I do not for one minute mean to say that education is everything; that a dishonest man who has no character is not more dangerous with a university education than if he did not have it. You have got to have a foundation of character in order to make education useful. Nor do I mean to say that speaking generally university education ought to be given to everybody. The State could not stand it. There is not enough money to bring it about, and if it were so, there would be a tendency, which frequently breaks up companies, of a desire for everybody to be a general. The great body of the negro race must always look forward, as, indeed, the great majority of the white race must always look forward, to hard manual labor as the means of livelihood, and I do not look upon that as a hard task to look forward to, either. When you work every day with your hands, you usually have a good digestion. That suggestion may not strike you as very important, but if you had to eat at as many banquets as I do you would appreciate it. Happiness is not in the luxuries of life after all. Real happiness is in the consciousness of having done the best you could with the material that the Lord has furnished you to work with; with having brought up your families in the best way you could; with having instilled in your children principles of morality, and with going down to your death with a reputation and a character that your families are proud of. Therefore, when one says that a majority of the negro race and a majority of the white race are destined to earn their livelihood in the sweat of their brow, one does not say that happiness is to be unevenly distributed. I guess if we had two or three millions of dollars and had the burden of taking care of it, and knowing where to give it in order that it might do good, we would conclude that there are some responsibilities that seem light to us, now that we do not have them, that might not be so easy if we had to discharge them. Perhaps the office of President of the United States might not seem quite so pleasant to you if I could take you aside and tell you some of the burdens connected with it. In other words, happiness is relative. It is comparative, but generally—I do not mean to say that there are not instances of sorrow, of illness and of unhappiness that seem to be thrust on men that make an exception—the happiness of a man is largely in himself, in his adopting proper methods of life and in his following the philosophy and the rules that his conscience teach him. In other words, we come back to the proposition that the Lord helps them that help themselves.

Of course, the education which you most need in this country, as indeed we need it in the North, is thorough primary and industrial education for everybody. I know enough about statistics to know that figures do lie; that it is easy to make a showing with respect to educational institutions and the spread of education that, when one investigates, the facts are not found justified. All through the Southern States, and, indeed, the Northern States—more in the South perhaps than in the North, because of the great poverty that visited the South immediately after the War—there is room for tremendous improvement in the system of education, especially in the rural districts. We have had occasion to look into the matter as trustees of the Jeanes fund of a million dollars, and I hope considerably more than that, the income of which is to be used to increase the salaries and the character of the teaching, and to increase the length of the time of the colored rural public schools in the South. We do not expect that that million dollars is going to aid a great number of little negroes, but what we hope to do is to make such investigations, to make such reports and to make such progress where we do spend the money as to furnish an opportunity for public authorities who are anxious to help on the cause of education, to ascertain the defects in the present system and the places where money can be spent to elevate and make that system better.

Such a school as this is an inspiration. This school, Hampton School, and the school at Tuskegee, are all instances of what one man or one woman can effect; that at Hampton, General Armstrong, a white man; that at Tuskegee, Booker Washington, a colored man; here, Miss Laney, a colored woman. Of course, public education must ultimately depend upon taxation. There are school funds on a private foundation, many of them, and amounting to many millions of dollars, but ultimately a system of education, to be generally effective, must rest on taxation, and therefore you must depend on what your State and local governments ultimately shall give you.

Now, I verily believe that among those who are exercising authority in all the Southern States, there has been an agitation and a stirring up of the question of better education in such a way as to work for the benefit of the colored man and the white man. The truth is that there is a great improvement possible in the education of the white children of the South. The colored people are not the only ones who are suffering from insufficient education in that way; and perhaps the white people of the South have some reason to complain that those of us of the North devote especial attention to the colored children; but in the end we are all working for the same purpose—that is, we are working to make and create better individual character. You cannot improve a race *en masse.* You cannot take 25,000 negroes and make them better by a decree, or by shoving them through some sort of a mold. You have got to make them better by training each individual mind and soul in that 25,000. Those of us who have had political responsibilities sometimes feel and realize that.

The advance of the colored race depends upon the development of the individual, and the great encouragement that one finds here in this meeting today and in similar meetings in similar institutions is that we find the shining and needed example in the very person whose work this institution is.

21

The Uniting of Whites and Negroes

Delivered at Pelican Park, New Orleans, Louisiana, February 12, 1909

Mr. Jones and My Colored Fellow-citizens:

I thank the Committee of Arrangements, of which Mr. Werlein, who has already addressed you, was one of the chiefs, for giving me an opportunity to meet you this morning. I should not feel that I had performed my duty in coming into a community in which the colored people form so important a part unless I had an opportunity to meet them and speak to them.

I wish, first, to apologize for my tardiness. That is one of those rare blessings. Not to be tardy, but to be prompt, is one of those small virtues that, nevertheless, enter into the success of life, and I do not wish by my example to interfere with the progress of anybody else by encouraging that sin, but if you had a Committee of the Progressive Union arranging a good many things for you to do, and if you were trying to form a Cabinet, to prepare an inaugural address, and to get over the effects of sitting up pretty late at night as the result of New Orleans hospitality, perhaps you would be willing to forgive me.

I am glad to be here under the auspices of the colored Young Men's Christian Association, for I believe that Association, colored and white, to be one of the great instrumentalities in our civic community for helping young men in the path of rectitude and virtue. And those of us who have been young men know that we cannot have too many instrumentalities of that sort. I should go on at some length and discuss the great results accomplished by that Association, not only in the cities of America and Europe, but in those dependencies in which we are greatly interested, in the far-distant islands in the Pacific, in Cuba, Porto Rico and on the Isthmus of Panama; but I have some other things to say this morning, and I close my reference to that Association by expressing my profound sympathy with its objects, and my desire, whenever occasion offers, to aid it in the great work in which it is engaged.

Now, I am going to make you a non-political talk this morning. I hope that I am to be the President of the people, and I hope that nothing that I shall say while a guest of a State and city, under non-political auspices, will be construed into a party or political reference. But there are certain propositions upon which members of different parties agree, and I am glad to know that from the speeches of this morning. In the first place, you are in America as a part of the American people. As the Reverend Mr. Walker, of your race, said in my presence in Augusta: "We feel very happy in the South, and there isn't any place between this and glory to which we wish to go from here."

Now, a reference was made in the very clear, lucid and beautiful address of welcome which we heard this morning to religion as an element in uplifting your race. I agree that it is a most important element. I agree, too, that your race is very subject to that influence. You are an emotional race. But I want to point out a difference between an emotional religion and a religion which stays. A man who loses himself in ecstasy in a prayer to God at night and the next morning spends all the family earnings at a saloon, possesses the kind of religion that does not work. I believe in work; faith is right, but works are necessary. And I believe, too, as you do, in the responsibility of the individual. I quite agree that, in our human eyes, the difference in burdens and in obstacles that individuals have to encounter, is very great, and that the man of wealth or the man born to luxury, ease and comfort, seems to have a great deal easier time than the man who has every temptation to steal and get along in any way because of the difficulties that are presented to him in life. Take the instance of the young man of wealth; how many young men who had a competence when they came to be twenty-one, do you know, who have accomplished anything in life? There are some, but you can count them on the fingers of your hand. Well, why is that? It is because it is so much easier to do nothing when you do not have to do anything that a man remains in a condition of no growth and stagnation, and as friction produces heat, it is obstacles overcome that make character. As for me, I would a good deal rather believe in the religious character of the man who saves his week's earnings and goes to church regularly than the man who is unctuous and talks loudly at prayer-meeting and yet lets his children go without comforts. Now, I am saying this because I believe that the virtues of thrift, economy and industry are the virtues that are going to rescue your race and put you on a level with progress and success. I believe that you have your own future to work out.

Now, with reference to the race question and race feeling in the South, I have this conviction: that we have made great progress in forty years. The work to this point has been hard and heartrending; and, at times, the agony of spirit has been very hard to bear, but as you look back over the last fifty years, as any one looks back over your history during that period, the progress that has been made is marked. Now, I say that not to make you conceited, not to swell your heads, but merely to give you encouragement, for I believe in encouragement.

Of course, a race of people, as an individual, can lessen its usefulness by getting an impression of individual importance, of individual ability, and by the fact that he is the only one in the community, but I have discovered in the history of your race that you have not been lacking in candid friends to tell you the latent defects of the race. That sort of candor can be overdone, and what you need is a clear, truthful statement of how you can work out your future by the practice of thrift and industry, by making yourselves useful in your community, and by that very usefulness compelling the respect you desire; and, on the other hand, not looking about for people to help you on with something you have not done. My own judgment is that we are reaching a point that, to those of us who believe the question can be settled, should be a great encouragement. What we of the North must avoid doing is to give the impression that we are in any way attempting to force a settlement. What we are to do is to stand by and encourage the movement of friendliness and mutual interest between the whites and the blacks. I do not like to criticize people. That is easy, but it does not help. But you can differ from people without criticizing them. One of the things that always strikes me with a little bit of amusement is the solemn consideration of difficult questions by people who offer a solution with tremendous earnestness by a proposal that no man, when he sits down to think it over, can regard as practical or possible. The proposition to which I refer is that the white and colored people cannot live together in the same community, and therefore we have got to move the colored people into a far distant land. Now, do you believe anybody, when he sits down and thinks about it, will regard that solution as possible? Well, of course he won't. You are here, ten million people, and where are we going to move you; how are we going to do it? And if we attempted to move you, the first persons who would protest are the people with whom it is said you cannot live in peace. It does not do any good to say that the race question is insoluble; that the two races cannot live together in the same community, because you are doing it. And we are getting along, and that is the problem we are to settle. There isn't any other problem before us. In other words, I would like to get down to hard tack and practical business in this matter, and that business I believe to be, as the gentleman who delivered the address of welcome said, the elevation of the individual; in his education and in his training and in those hardy virtues that tell of the standing of a people in a community. Now, advanced education is necessary in order to teach a comparatively few leaders of the race—professional men—but, of course, the great education that is needed for the colored people, as is needed for other people, is the practical education and the industrial education that shall fit their hands to progress, thrift, success and well-to-do character in the community.

I have been told in the address of welcome, and only want to comment and reiterate, that you are here in this community with the white man. That he has largely the wealth and largely the advantage of you in education. That you are necessary to him and he is necessary to you.

It gave me great pleasure to hear the Mayor of your city say that you are a law-abiding population. I believe the conditions prevailing between the two races in the South today and the earnest interest that the white man in the South is taking in your development are the great grounds for thinking that the race question is in process of settlement. You have got to know that you cannot, as a people, stand behind criminal lawlessness of any sort and receive the sympathy of the white people in the North or the white people in the South. You must condemn your own criminals with the same severity that you condemn white criminals. Now, I agree that that is difficult, because you have a history in which injustice has been shown to you, and you are naturally suspicious, when a man is condemned, that there may be race prejudice entering into the condemnation. That is an element of difficulty to eliminate, and yet you must eliminate it, and you must, if you would be American citizens, side with law and order against your own people as well as against a white ruffian. In other words, if you want a "square deal," you have got to give it. You cannot ask for justice on the one hand and then say you ought to be released from its enforcement on the other.

Now, my friends, I want to extend to you my earnest feeling of sympathy in your struggle onward and upward. I am greatly encouraged by the presence of such an audience as this, and of the school children, but, for the interest of your race, do not encourage them to believe that there is anything in the way of honest industry that is above them. Let them understand that labor is honorable; and that it does not make any difference how humble the character of labor, it dignifies the laborer; that if a boy has a high school education and cannot get any other work, it is honorable for him to go down in a ditch and work.

My friends, I tell you when a man comes to preach and sermonize, it is a little dangerous, and I am afraid, if I went on, I should continue in the same strain, when you might think I ought to change the subject. I only want to say again that it gratifies me to have had the opportunity, under the auspices of Dr. Jones, your chairman, whom I have known for years and value most highly, to be here; to have this talk with you and to give you encouragement, so far as I can give you encouragement, and I believe I can, in saying that the problem is working out in the South (there are theorists who say that it will never work out), and that it is working out by the cultivation of mutual good feeling and interest between the races in the South, and that we in the North are glad to stand by and help when we can, but we do not want to come in here and, by a process of action that shall arouse feeling against the object which we have in view, to mix up matters and deal with things that are better understood here. I thank you.

22

The Learned Professions and Political Government

Delivered at the University of Pennsylvania, Philadelphia,
Pennsylvania, February 22, 1909

Ladies and Gentlemen:

It is the duty of every citizen, no matter what his profession, business or trade, to give as much attention as he can to the public weal, and to take as much interest as he can in political matters. Americans generally have recognized these duties, and the result is that we find active in political life, prominent in the legislative and executive councils of the Government, men representing all professions, all branches of business and all trades. Perhaps the expression "representing" is not fortunate, because they are not elected by guilds, or professions or crafts, and they do not represent their fellows in the sense of being required to look after their peculiar interests. What I mean is that among public men who enact laws and enforce them may be found those who in early life at least have had experience in every business, every craft and every profession.

Nevertheless, as political and governmental necessities change, they have a tendency to increase the number taken from one profession or another for reasons that can be distinctly traced; and I propose this morning

The next profession for consideration in its relation to Governmental matters is that of medicine. Until very recently its influence has been practically nothing in a professional way. There have been physicians who have given up their practice and gone into politics; but there was some trait of theirs adapted to success in politics that had little or nothing to do with the practice of their profession.

They have become more interested in government of late years because the functions of government have widened, and now embrace in a real and substantial way the preservation of the health of all the people. The effect which imperfect drainage, bad water, impure food, ill-ventilated houses and a failure to isolate contagion have in killing people has become more and more apparent with the study which great sanitary authorities have given to the matter and has imposed much more distinctly and unequivocally the burden upon municipal, State and Federal Government of looking after the public health. The expansion of our Government into the tropics, the necessity for maintaining our armies and navies there and of supporting a great force of workmen in the construction of such an enterprise as that of the Panama Canal, have greatly exalted the importance of the discoveries of the medical profession in respect to the prevention and cure of human disease and of diseases of domestic animals.

The triumph which has been reached in the name of the medical profession in the discovery as to the real causes of yellow fever and malaria, and the suppression of those diseases by killing or preventing the propagation or the infection of the mosquito is one of the wonders of human progress. It has made the construction of the Panama Canal possible. It has rendered life in the tropics for immigrants from the temperate zone consistent with health and reasonable length of life, and it has opened possibilities in the improvement of the health and strength of tropical races themselves under governmental teaching, assistance and supervision that were unthought of two decades ago.

Sanitary engineering, with its proper treatment of water making it wholesome and harmless with its removal of the filth and sewage and its conversion of what was noxious into most useful agencies, confirms the governmental importance of the professions of medicine and the kindred technical professions of chemistry, engineering and all branches of physical research.

So marked has been this increase in the importance of the medical profession in governmental agencies that the doctors themselves have organized a movement for the unification of all agencies in the Federal Government used to promote the public health in one bureau or department, at the head of which they wish to put a man of their own or kindred branch of science.

How near this movement will come in accomplishing the complete purpose of its promoters only the National Legislature can tell. Certainly the economy of the union of all health agencies of the National Government in one bureau or department is wise. Whether at the head of that department should be put a doctor of medicine or some other person must depend on the individual and not on his technical professional learning or skill. It is the capacity to organize, coordinate and execute that is needed at the head of a department and not so much deep or broad technical and professional skill. It is the ability to judge whether others have such technical or professional skill that the head of the department who makes the selection of the members of his department should be endowed with.

However this may be, it is becoming more and more clear that the extending of governmental duties into a territory covered by the profession of medicine is bringing physicians more and more into political and governmental relation, and we may expect that in the next decade they will play a far greater part than they have heretofore; and it is proper that they should.

I may stop here and mention other technical professions, like those of the chemist, soil expert, botanist, horticulturist, forester, meteorologist and the student of general agricultural science, all of whom must be consulted and have been consulted in the improvement of our agriculture, and in that movement generally characterized as a conservation of our natural resources. The waste which is going on today in our forest, water and soil supplies has been brought to the attention of the public in startling statistics by the President and the commission whose report he has transmitted to Congress, and such conservation may well be considered with conservation of human life, in the progress of governmental sanitation, hygiene and the preventives and cure of disease by quarantine and health regulations.

We must look in the future to great development in all these branches and to prominence in political power and authority of those who shall succeed in effecting a reduction in the loss of human life from preventable disease and a saving of the national resources.

The Department of Agriculture is expanding in its usefulness and in the scope of its functions, and exercises a power directly beneficial to the production and sale of farm products and the profit of the farmer that no one could have anticipated at the time of its creation and organization. This will bring even more into political prominence than heretofore the scientific farmer generally familiar with the needs of agriculture throughout the country and able to understand the intricacies of the policy of foreign governments in the admission and exclusion of our farm products.

We come finally to the profession of the law. With the exception, perhaps, of the profession of arms, law has always been in all countries most prominent in political and governmental matters. This is so because in a wide sense the profession of the law is the profession of government, or at least it is the profession in the course of which agencies of the Government are always used, and in which the principles applied are those which effect either the relations between individuals or the relation between the Government and individuals, and all of which are defined by what, for the want of a better term, is called "municipal law."

It is natural that those whose business it is to construe laws, and whose profession it is to know what existing law is, should be called upon in the framing of new laws, to act an important part. It was natural that the framers of the Constitution, which was to be the fundamental law of the land, and to embody the limitations upon the central Government, deemed necessary in favor of the separate States, should be those who knew the laws of the separate States and who had the professional capacity of drafting written laws.

The creative function of the lawyer, as distinguished from his analytical function, is to put in written and legal form the intention of the person or persons which he wishes to make effective; if it be that of a people, through the Legislature, then in the form of a statute; if it be that of an agreement of individuals, then in the form of a written contract; if it be the desire of the executive, then in the form of an executive order, he must analyze the purpose of those for whom he acts and then be the careful draftsman of the instrument which shall correctly and truly embody that purpose.

Thus it has been that in all conventions, in all legislatures, in the great majority of public offices we find the lawyers to have been selected to carry on governmental work, and this has not been alone due to their knowledge of the law and their training in the drafting and forming of legal expression of the public will, but also in the fact that the necessities of their profession require them constantly to practise the temporary acquisition of technical knowledge of all other professions and all other businesses in order that they may properly present in forensic controversies the issues involved, or in negotiations involving technical matters may be sufficiently advised of the general principles of other professions and business to enable them correctly to interpret and embody the result of the negotiation in language that shall express the meaning of the parties.

To put it in a different way, the business of the lawyer is not only to fight lawsuits, but it is to tell the people who desire to accomplish certain results how such results can legally be accomplished, and by writing and instruction to bring about such results under the forms of law. This is executive.

In other words, this executive faculty is a very marked necessity in the successful practice of the modern lawyer. With him the power of imitation and of devising the methods of accomplishment are frequently the secret of his professional success.

Of course, a great advocate is a great lawyer. In the presentation of the case of the controversy to court, there is called out his power of lucid statement, of analysis and of forceful presentation of the arguments in favor of his client, and the great judge is ordinarily the great analyst, who with common sense and the judicial quality has the proper sense of proportion, which enables him to weigh and decide in favor of the better reason.

But the lawyer, and especially the modern lawyer, whose business is in organizing corporations and partnerships, in the setting going of enterprises, has the counterpart of these functions to perform, and that is the power of initiation, of drawing contracts and of drafting statutes to effect the purpose either of his client or the people as his duty may be.

Now, I am far from being blind to the defects and weaknesses of the profession of the law, of which I once had the honor to be a member. Lawyers are frequently a conservative class. They adhere to the things that are, simply because they are, and reluctantly admit the necessity for change.

When the business community yields to temptation and goes into practices that have an evil tendency, members of the profession are always found who, for professional compensation, can be induced to promote the success of such business methods; and the combinations to regulate the output and control of prices of various classes of merchandise, and to stifle competition by methods which have had statutory denunciation, and which it has been the purpose of the National Administration to restrain, repress and stamp out, could only have been as powerful and successful as they have been through the manipulation, acuteness and creative faculty of members of the legal profession.

But on the other hand, when statutory reforms are to be effected, especially in business methods and by introducing limitations upon the use of private property, so as to stamp out the evil involved in combinations of capital, and at the same time not destroy that enormous benefit inuring to the public and insuring commercial progress of such combinations, the work of drafting the statutes and enforcing them, so as to secure higher and better business methods without impairing the means of business progress, must ultimately fall to the members of the legal profession.

It is members of that profession in the Supreme Court who are to determine whether such limitations are within the constitutional power of Congress. It is the members of the legal profession in the trial courts and the Supreme Courts that are to construe the statutes and enforce the ultimate penalties for their violation. It must be, not wholly, but chiefly, members of the legal profession that shall draft the amendments to the Federal and State statutes which shall give such organization and efficiency to government machinery on the one hand and such clear definition of the limitations of the combinations of capital on the other, that shall uphold legitimate business progress on the one hand and strike down vicious abuses on the other. Hence it is today, no less than at the foundation of our Government, the profession of the law is the most important in its relation to politics and political government.

It is said that business men have more executive capacity, and, being at the head of large business concerns, have had more experience in dealing with large transactions and in directing the movements of many men. This is doubtless true in a sense. The real executive faculty is so rare that it makes itself conspicuous in whatever profession or business it may appear. But I must think that the practice of the law, especially in what I have previously described as the creative part of the practice, brings a lawyer into relation with other men in such a directing and instructing way that he is himself a constant cultivator of the executive faculty.

More than this, business men carry on their business according to their own rules. Great government departments have to be carried on under statutes and legal regulations with many detailed sections and provisions, and every departmental head must study and analyze the statutes and regulations which control it with care in order not to be a violator of the law. This necessity for analysis of the rules governing the conduct of a department makes its administration much easier for a lawyer than for a business man or a member of any other profession.

In what I have said I have not argued that the lawyer is necessarily the leader in public opinion, the exponent of great reform, or that he is likely to fix the standards of public opinion in a moral awakening and an uplift of business integrity. Such leaders and exponents of great moral reforms are essential to our progress. They come from every profession and walk in life. They are born leaders of men.

The mercantile spirit, the effect of luxurious living, the greed of financial power, the inertia produced by present comfort, all have a tendency to blind us to abuses and evils that creep into our business, governmental and social life, and it needs some great, strong, courageous spirit to paint, in not too delicate color and with no fear of hurting people's feelings, the truth, and to stir up the people to demand in tones that cannot be denied a reform of the abuses.

After it is settled by popular decree that such reforms must take place, it is for the members of the legal profession, clearly advised as to the necessities of the case, having a nice and accurate knowledge of the operation of proposed statutes and clearly perceiving the practical difficulties in their enforcement which must be obviated by special provision, to furnish the legal means of making such reforms permanent and effective.

National exigency seems to call forth, as if by aid of a special providence, the men peculiarly fitted to meet the requirements of the situation. Such were Lincoln and Grant during the great Civil War. Such in the Revolution was Washington, the anniversary of whose birthday this University appropriately makes its festal day.

He was not a lawyer or a doctor or a minister. He was a surveyor and farmer; as a student of military science only in the hard school of experience, his profession may be said to have been that of arms. Not brilliant, not facile, not eloquent, he had those qualities which placed him far above the brilliant, facile, able and learned men who were gathered about him in the struggle for American independence. He was a leader of men. His pure, disinterested patriotism, his freedom from small jealousies, his marvelous common sense, his indomitable perseverance and patience and his serenity and calm under the most trying circumstances, gave him the victory—a victory which could be traced not to brilliant genius or professional training, but to that which of all things is the most to be pursued and desired—to his high character as a man.

23

A Cheerful Review of Negro Activities

Delivered, under the Auspices of the Armstrong Association and in Aid of Hampton Institute, at Carnegie Hall, New York, New York, February 23, 1909

Mr. Chairman, Ladies and Gentlemen:

We have ten millions of Negroes in the United States and of that ten million I suppose nine millions live in the Southern States. Now, if you read the Congressional Record—I remember one distinguished Senator wanted to compel the public to read it—and there is a great deal of very useful learning in it—there is a great deal you can sympathize with in it and a great deal of truth and a good deal of humor; that is, it awakens your humor, sometimes in sympathy, and sometimes at it.

Now if you study the Congressional Record you will see that there are some statesmen that say it is impossible for the Negro and the white races to live together; that the solution is beyond the hope of human effort. Well, the ten millions are here and what are you going to do about it? There are some who propose that we should move them bodily out of the country. They do not say where, they do not say how and they do not when, but out of the country they are to go. And when there is an attempt to move five hundred of them out of the State in which it is said their relations to the whites are most inharmonious, you have a riot the minute you propose to move them, on the part of and by the very men with whom they cannot live.

It seems to me that that is the *reductio ad absurdum* with reference to a suggestion that expatriation is a solution of this question. The solemn, scientific statement of a man that the races cannot live together, even though it appear in a Congressional Record, ought not to occupy our minds for a moment, because they are living together and they have lived together for over a hundred years. Now, the question is whether we or they or all of us together can make that living together better for both races. It is a problem that is set before us and it does not help us to say that you cannot work it out, because we have got to work it out.

A race feeling, a race prejudice is a fact and a man who does not recognize it is just exactly as illogical as the man who says that ten millions of people now in the country cannot live with the other seventy millions that are here, when they are living there. It is a race feeling, and you cannot dispose of it by saying that it ought not to exist. It does exist, and that is part of the problem.

Now, how are you going to wipe it out to the extent of making it so that it shall not produce injustice and a lack of harmony between the races? Well, I think you are going to work it out. I believe in my heart that you are going to work it out by making it to the advantage and profit of both races to see that it is not to the advantage of either to allow that race feeling to continue between them to the extent of making it difficult for them to live together.

The Negro is absolutely essential to the development of the South. His labor the South needs, and the more you instruct that labor the more valuable he becomes to the South. Hence it is that the work of Hampton Institute has its intrinsic importance. It is the solution of the race question. I do not believe, and I do not think most men believe in too many crutches for people that are trying to learn to walk. But if you furnish them just enough education to know how to use their minds and their hands and their legs in productive occupations you give them the instrument by which they can help themselves, and then if they are a race that has the spirit to help themselves the future is before them and the opportunity is theirs.

I do not profess to know as much about the Negro question—of course not—as these gentlemen who have spoken before me, but I have given a good deal of attention to the matter; I have studied the statistics of the growth of the race; I have studied the amount of property that the race has accumulated, the reduction in the percentage of illiteracy, the amount of products brought forth under the hand of the Negro laborer and the Negro farmer in the South; and I say that no unprejudiced person can read those statistics without marveling that the Negro race has made the progress that it has made in the last fifty years under the burdens and obstacles that it has had to meet. They show self-initiation; they show self-help. Why, a race that produces a Booker Washington in a century ought to feel confident that it can do miracles in time.

I have been South recently. If you credit Brother Washington's story you will think I have made some sort of an impression there. I do not remember that particular auntie but I know they have aunties in that country who know how to attract one to regular meals.

There were a number of things that were brought home to me with much more emphasis on account of my visit than they ever had been before. One afternoon I drove out with a Southern lady and gentleman who said that they wanted to show me the inside of what I had seen in riding about the country: the Shiloh Orphanage—printed in letters that indicated that the man who had handled the brush was not an artist. We went in there and we found a colored man, I should think about sixty years of age, the perfect image of Uncle Tom in Uncle Tom's Cabin, and he and his wife had taken an old farm with a lot of outbuildings on it and had gathered in there all the little Negro waifs of the town of Augusta and he was bringing them up to useful jobs, trusting from week to week to get enough to feed those children and to clothe them. He took us into a room that would not have met the requirements of the modern school superintendent with reference to cubic feet of air or ventilation, but there he gathered his thirty or forty nondescript Negro children, boys and girls of different ages, and he had them repeat the Twenty-third Psalm and then recite. Then he told them to "get up and be polite" and they got up and all bowed to us and said they were glad to see us—in unison—and I asked him how he got along. Well, he said, it was pretty hard work sometimes but they raised their own chickens and they had some cows and they sold milk and they sold eggs and they did what they could and the neighbors helped some. It was really a most pathetic scene. I tried to be as dignified as I could but I did need my handkerchief before I got through.

Some of those who were there sent small checks to help the old man along; and the old man thought I was a little more useful than for merely three meals a day and he circulated the report that we had contributed something to his aid, and I just got a telegram today saying that he raised on the faith of that publication some three thousand dollars to pay off the mortgage on the old place and that he was going on with his useful work saving those waifs.

I instance that to show the spirit of initiation, the spirit of anxiety to do something for themselves that I saw among the Negroes in the South.

Then another time I had the privilege of going to an institution founded by a Miss Lucy Laney, a Negro woman, I should say now of some forty-five years. She has, I think, some five or six hundred students. They began with the wrong idea as to education, but now they have come to adopt the Hampton and the Tuskegee system and are teaching the girls who are there useful knowledge. I found myself on the platform with Mr. Robert C. Ogden and then I knew I was in the right place.

Now that woman, I think, was a graduate of Hampton, but I am not sure—[Mr. Washington: Of Atlanta University]—Atlanta University, and she has this great institution that she is carrying on, deriving money from some generous supporters in the North, but there is an instance of initiation, of self-help in the race that indicates that they are in favor of doing something themselves and they are not waiting to be helped along with crutches.

On the other hand, I rejoiced to find that that work had the sympathy of the Southern people of education and refinement and common sense.

It is very difficult to speak in parliamentary language of the advocacy of the doctrine that we are to keep the Negroes in ignorance. I think the statement refutes itself—and it does not awaken the sympathy of the intelligent South. One of the difficulties in the South is that it is not the Negroes only that need education; and I mean that literally. The number of ignorant among the whites is enough to call properly for the attention of our citizens to reduce the illiteracy and increase by industrial and other education their ability to be good citizens in the community.

Now we sometimes get information and aid from sources that we would hardly expect. I think the history of the improvement of the civil service of England is that it came by way of India. And the history of the improvement in practical education in this country, in industrial education, is that it came through Hampton, through General Armstrong, in teaching the colored students and the Indians, and that now we all over the North and the South are profiting by the thousands that he taught in that Institute.

General Armstrong was a great man and the generations will rise and call him blessed. He taught the secret that will solve the race question in the South. The truth is that the success of Hampton and of Tuskegee is doing great good for the ignorant Southern white children.

I remember Mr. Dillard at the North Carolina dinner told this story: He said that they were introducing some Italians into the South and an old darkey inquired who those immigrants were, and they said that they were Italians that were coming there. He shook his head and said, "Well, I don't know how that will be, we's niggers has hard enough time to support the whites that are here."

Now, I do not agree with that authority. I think that it will help the South to have immigration. I believe in competition in labor as in everything else, and we have found on the Isthmus of Panama that our West Indian Negroes work a great deal better and do a great deal more satisfactory work, now that we have introduced Spaniards, Italians and Greeks, and I do not think it would hurt at all.—There is room enough in the South for all of them.—The resources of the South are only scratched and if they go there it will help the Negro.

I think it is pretty hard to appeal always to a New York audience and a Boston audience for charitable contributions. I think the West ought to pay part of this work that is done for the benefit of the whole country and I hope that meetings of this kind may be held in Cincinnati and Chicago and other places and that such pictures as we have had tonight may be presented to those audiences in order to make them be generous and just.

It is true that the ancestors of the Negroes today were brought here against their will. They are Americans; they are entitled to our aid and sympathy. This is the only country and the only home they know. Ours is the only flag they can live under and it is a flag they have shown themselves willing to die for.

I should feel very much discouraged if I did not believe that the Negro was going to work out his own salvation. I believe it from what I have already said and I have had the pleasure of addressing a number of Negro audiences in the South. I remember one audience, a Young Men's Christian Association audience, where Rev. Dr. Walker, one of the most eloquent men, black or white, testified to the harmony that existed between the two races. He said we are happy here. He said, "This is the only place we want to live in until we go to Glory," and, said he, "we propose to stay here until we do go to Glory."

Now the great aid, the man who is able to assist more than we can, even though we contribute our money, is the Southern white man, and as it is to his profit and as he grows more intelligent to see what the good of the country is he will certainly see that it is to his advantage to have the Negro increase in intelligence, in providence and in industry—I do not see why we may not reasonably take courage and believe that the elements are there in the South together to work out this problem and to uplift this race to a moral and to a spiritual plane that will insure its happiness.

No man can conceive the humiliation and the agony of spirit that the Negroes have to suffer in their struggle upward when they encounter the race feeling and the injustices to which it leads. But it may help them, I hope it will, to give them stronger character, and there is a future before them that, if they overcome these obstacles, is well worth the effort. Personally, I think it is one of the great problems that we have before us in this country. I believe in the ultimate justice of all the American people. I believe also in their good sense, and when a policy involves justice and good sense I think the American people can be trusted to urge that policy and to carry it on to its ultimate conclusion.

One of the things that a man who hasn't any money is able to do is to advise the man who has, what to do with it. I know that, changing the situation somewhat, a man who has not to appoint a Cabinet certainly knows how to appoint it, for I have had a great deal of advice on that subject; but I do think that there is nothing that offers such an opportunity for the men of this country who have money and do not know what to do with it as the cause of the Negro industrial education in the South, and I agree with the last speaker that it does not speak well for the intelligence of those who have had money to distribute that Hampton is now seeking two millions of dollars as an endowment and that Tuskegee needs as much more, when both institutions have demonstrated their usefulness and have shown that they offer the only remedy for the solution of one of the greatest questions that has ever presented itself to the American people. I thank you.